EASY

COMPOST

The Secret
to
Great Soil
and
Spectacular
Plants

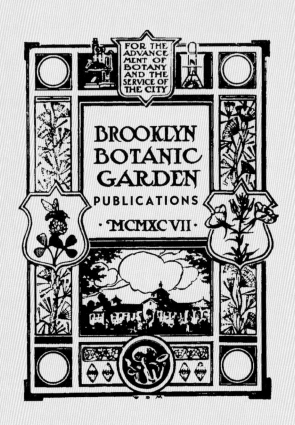

FOR THE
ADVANCE
MENT OF
BOTANY
AND THE
SERVICE OF
THE CITY

BROOKLYN
BOTANIC
GARDEN
PUBLICATIONS
· MCMXCVII ·

Janet Marinelli
SERIES EDITOR

Beth Hanson
MANAGING EDITOR

Bekka Lindstrom
ART DIRECTOR

Stephen K-M. Tim
VICE PRESIDENT, SCIENCE, LIBRARY & PUBLICATIONS

Judith D. Zuk
PRESIDENT

Elizabeth Scholtz
DIRECTOR EMERITUS

EASY

COMPOST

The Secret to Great Soil and Spectacular Plants

Beth Hanson⁄Editor

Technical consulting provided by Patricia Jasaitis & Benjamin Grant
of Brooklyn Botanic Garden's Urban Composting Project,
an educational initiative funded by the
New York City Department of Sanitation

Handbook #153

Handbooks in the 21st⁄Century Gardening Series, formerly Plants & Gardens,
are published quarterly at 1000 Washington Ave., Brooklyn, NY 11225.
Subscription included in Brooklyn Botanic Garden subscriber membership dues ($35.00 per year).
ISSN # 0362⁄5850 ISBN # 1⁄889538⁄03⁄5
Printed by Science Press, a division of the Mack Printing Group

Table of Contents

INTRODUCTION

Why Compost?

BY BETH HANSON

IRECENTLY READ somewhere that by incorporating just one generous dose of compost into your garden's soil, you are adding as much topsoil as it would take nature a century to accumulate. Considering the little bit of effort that is required to compost and to dig the finished product into the soil, this is an incredible payback.

If this isn't a compelling enough reason to start composting, consider these: New research is proving what many gardeners have long intuited—compost helps protect plants from diseases and insect pests. Compost enhances the soil's ability to hold water and air, both essential for plants. Over time, compost-amended soil darkens and warms up more quickly in the spring, extending your growing season. Unlike soluble chemical fertilizers, compost releases its nutrients slowly as plants need them. And by composting, you can put your kitchen and garden scraps to good use—much better than landfilling.

As you'll discover in the pages ahead, composting can be as big or little an undertaking as you like. For some composters, the process becomes a passionate pursuit; they are forever in search of the recipe and method that will reward them with a humus-laden compost in the least amount of time. Other composters have a spot where they dump leaves and prunings as they rake or clip, and once in a while they'll pull some finished—also humus-laden—stuff

By adding just one generous dose of compost into your garden's soil, you are adding as much topsoil as it would take nature a century to accumulate.

from the bottom of the heap. But like me, most composters fall somewhere between these groups. We keep a container on the kitchen counter for coffee grounds and carrot peelings, and when they become odoriferous, we dump them on the pile, mixing them with the twigs, weeds, leaves and old blossoms already heaped there. We turn the pile when we remember to, and are gratified to find that while we weren't looking, worms, bacteria, fungi and other creatures have transformed our organic waste into a treat for the soil and the plants.

The multitudinous creatures in the pile, members of the "decomposer food web," are the reason that composting works so well. In a hot pile, one where the balance of carbon- to nitrogen-rich materials and air to moisture are just right, life explodes. Protozoa and bacteria absorb nutrients from the moist medium around them, and flourish. These one-celled creatures are preyed upon by nematodes (roundworms); some fungi snare nematodes in traps along their strands and consume them, and the fungi, in turn, are fed upon by mites. As they munch their way through the pile and through each other, these decomposers release energy and nutrients from organic materials, making compost the incredible stuff that it is.

You may have begun hearing about composting in the last couple of decades as the organic gardening movement has burgeoned, but for eons, people who lived off the land understood the salubrious properties of compost. As you'll read in the following chapter, by husbanding all their organics—including "night-soil" or sewage—and composting these using various techniques, Chinese farmers have managed to keep their fields fertile for thousands of years; they are so successful that they now feed 22 percent of the world's population on just 7 percent of the globe's arable land.

If, like the Chinese, you are challenged for space, don't despair. You can compost on a spot as small as a windowsill, and use the finished product on your houseplants. On the following pages you can learn about this and other ways to "micro-compost." If, as is more likely, you're going to compost in the backyard, you'll learn where to build your pile, what to put in it and lots of ingenious composting techniques. You'll even find complete plans for two compost bins—one of them a compost bench that doubles as a retreat in the garden—designed by staff of the Brooklyn Botanic Garden Urban Composting Project and architect Jeff Wilkinson.

What could be more gratifying than recycling all the "waste" from your yard and kitchen and doing so in a way that enhances the earth. In fact I can't think of any reason why you shouldn't compost—so start reading, then start piling.

COMPOSTING'S HISTORY

From The Odyssey to an Industry

BY BENJAMIN GRANT

HUMANS HAVE LONG UNDERSTOOD that all living matter returns to the earth. Decay and death are as fundamental as growth and life, and together they form the most basic ecological process: the continual recycling of organic matter. People have sought to manage this process for their own benefit for as long as they have been aware of it. Composting, one method of channeling decay, allows the gardener or farmer to enrich the soil to insure its long-term bounty.

LEARNING THE CYCLE

The earliest agricultural civilizations arose in river valleys. Their soils' fertility depended on the natural influx of silt brought by floodwaters. Before long, early agriculturists also discovered the beneficial effects of animal manure, which remained the most important agricultural fertilizer well into the 20th century.

While the use of manure as a fertilizer was widespread throughout the ancient world, the first written record of it comes from the Akkadian empire, about 2300 B.C. Later, in *The Odyssey,* Homer describes the stockpiling of manures for agricultural purposes. Homer's countrymen, the citizens of Athens, sold their sewage to farmers for use as a fertilizer and got it to the fields in a system of ditches.

The Romans experimented widely, composting a variety of materials, and even heated their vegetable beds in winter with steaming piles of manure. Over time,

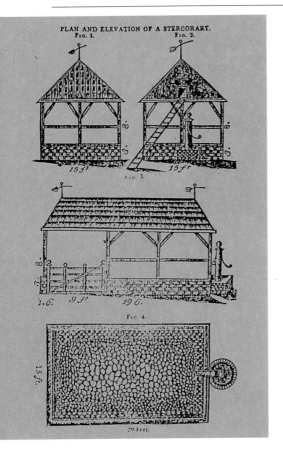

PLAN AND ELEVATION OF A STERCORARY.

George Washington composted manure in his "stercorary"; his original conception (left) and the remains today (above).

manure composting became a fundamental part of European agriculture. The technique is also prominent in the agricultural writings of Arab civilizations. Even the Talmud offers an injunction to handle only well-aged—composted—manures.

AGRARIAN IDEALISTS IN EARLY AMERICA

The Europeans who came to the New World found indigenous peoples who had some things to teach them about how to make the most of organic matter. One of the earliest stories of the American colonists features Squanto, a Native American who showed the colonists how burying a fish in the ground with corn seeds would provide the plant with important nutrients. But careful attention to soil fertility was more the exception than the rule in colonial America.

Though a landed yeomanry was generally thought to be the backbone of the nascent republic, American farmers' agricultural practices apparently were shoddy. Two well-known exceptions, George Washington and Thomas Jefferson—both leaders in more ways than one—experimented extensively with composting on their own land. Washington devoted an outbuilding at Mt. Vernon, called a "stercorary," to manure collection and composting. Jefferson also saved manure and gathered "muck," the rich anaerobic soil of swamps, to mix with it.

In the late 18th century, agricultural essayist John Taylor bemoaned the state of American agricultural practice in a series of influential essays on manuring. British author William Cobbett derided sloppy American gardening as a symptom of moral weakness while George Washington Carver, a great proponent of composting, urged farmers to use their free time to lay in organic materials. Each of these writers and thinkers viewed proper stewardship of the land as the basis of civic and moral virtue.

TRADITIONAL AGRICULTURE IN ASIA

Jefferson would probably have admired the farmers of East Asia, many of whom work some of the world's oldest continually cultivated fields. Parts of China have been densely planted for 4,000 years with no apparent loss of fertility. The secret? Continual and intensive application of organic material to the fields. Farmers using one traditional Chinese method of composting grow a legume cover crop, harvest it and mix it with dredged river silt in a pit where the mixture composts. It is then applied to the land.

To this day the Chinese see manures and organic wastes as valuable resources and carefully husband them. Somewhat less tasteful to Western sensibilities is the extensive use throughout Asia of night-soil, or sewage, as a fertilizer. Unlike people in the West, the Chinese don't think of sewage as a liability but as an asset. In 1908 the city of Shanghai was paid the then whopping sum of $31,000 by a private hauler for rights to the city's sewage.

These days Asian farmers stabilize sewage in impermeable tanks, then judiciously apply it to crops, turning what is one of the West's most expensive and challenging disposal problems into an economic boon. As one contemporary Chinese agronomist put it: "Of great surprise and concern to the Chinese when they visit [the West] is the failure to use human and animal excretions and to consider them as troublesome wastes. This to the Chinese is an extreme extravagance."

Despite the widespread availability of "modern" agricultural chemicals and techniques in China, nearly half of the nutrients applied to the land are from organic sources.

THE CHEMICAL MOVEMENT AND THE ORGANIC MOVEMENT

Before chemical fertilizers became available in the late 19th century, American farmers used a variety of industrial wastes and by-products as agricultural fertilizers, including cotton-seed meal, municipal garbage, seaweed, fish, crab and lobster waste, hoof-and-horn meal and blood meal.

By the early 20th century, however, chemical fertilizers had become as important as their organic counterparts, and soon eclipsed them. A 1914 fertilizer handbook lists 55 organic fertilizers, manures and cover crops, and as many chemical preparations. A similar book put out in 1979 does not mention a single organic fertilizer.

Throughout the century, the chemical revolution has marched forward, but some agriculturists have not forgotten the benefits of organic matter. The father of the organic movement, Sir Albert Howard, was a government agronomist in India and Kenya in the 1930s. While stationed abroad he experimented with plants and soil, and became convinced that the key to healthy crops is healthy soil, which needs the benefit not only of the nutrients that chemicals could provide, but of abundant organic matter and living organisms as well. Howard developed the Indore method of composting (named for a locality in India), the most controlled and effective composting method to date; it stressed a careful mix of ingredients to insure the best retention of nutrients. His ideas and techniques spread quickly throughout the world.

A few years later, J.I. Rodale began publishing *Organic Farming and Gardening* in the U.S. and soon became the best known proponent of the organic movement, encouraging several generations of gardeners to focus on composting as the key to a healthy, vital garden. As awareness of environmental issues has spread in recent years, the popularity of organic methods has surged, both in backyard gardens and in commercial agriculture. Meanwhile, a new set of motivations for composting has emerged.

GARBAGE

American municipalities produce almost 200 million tons of mixed residential garbage each year, most of which is landfilled. Sixty-eight percent of that material is organic (yard, food, paper and wood waste); this one-way stream of organic material makes its way from soil to crop to landfill. Many older landfills are reaching capacity and closing, and strict environmental regulations, the scarcity of land near urban areas and the opposition of local communities have all contributed to the increasing costs of new sites. Composting, for generations seen primarily as a way to create agricultural fertilizer, has been getting attention as a waste-reduction technique, and along with recycling, is diverting more and more organics from landfills.

Over millennia, the Chinese have applied compost to their lands; many fields remain fertile after 4,000 years of cultivation.

Most large-scale facilities compost yard waste, which is easily handled, usually separated from other garbage and plentiful enough that collection is generally worthwhile. A number of states, counties and municipalities have gone as far as outlawing the landfilling of yard waste in an effort to reduce disposal costs. About 3,500 yard-waste composting facilities are now in operation, some as private businesses, some as public services. Some municipalities, including Philadelphia and Milwaukee, now routinely compost dewatered sewage sludge (hats off to the Far East). Certain industrial organics, such as brewery and food-processing wastes, fish-processing residuals, and hundreds of "morts"—poultry carcasses—generated each day at industrial poultry farms, are also composted in some places.

Collecting compostables can be a challenge for municipalities, in part because homeowners produce food waste in small quantities and it quickly becomes unsavory. So instead of collection, many cities are taking a decentralized approach, giving away or subsidizing large numbers of backyard compost bins, and offering instruction and support.

Composting is coming full circle, as farmers and gardeners once again acknowledge the complexities and needs of soil. We have begun to recall what has been understood for millennia: that the earth does not give unconditionally or indefinitely, and that we must return what we take away.

NOURISHING THE EARTH

THAT NOURISHES US

How Compost Builds the Soil

BY GRACE GERSHUNY

FEED THE SOIL, NOT THE PLANT. According to this fundamental principle of organic crop nutrition, soil is a living community that requires nurture. And well-nurtured soil in turn nurtures the plants that are part of it. The primary food that soil needs is organic matter, and compost is the best way to provide it. You can feed plants through other means, but giving your soil compost is like feeding your family bread instead of a pile of flour and water, which after all contains the same nutrients.

WHAT IS COMPOST?

Soil health is indivisible from humus, the main component of compost. If a soil's fauna is vital and active, it will go to work breaking down raw organic matter—the waste products or remains of other organisms. Once organic matter has undergone some degree of decomposition, it can become humus, a dark brown, porous, spongy, somewhat gummy and pleasantly earthy-smelling substance.

Humus is actually a generic term for a substance that varies widely in its chemical characteristics, depending on the nature of the original material and the conditions of its decomposition. Each kind of humus is a complex mixture of biochemical compounds in a colloidal or gel-like form, including plant waxes and lignins, and the gums and starches transformed by bacteria and fungi as they

14

Compost is the ultimate all-around garden elixir. It increases the amount of air and water that's available to plants, releases nutrients as plants need them, and promotes plants' resistance to diseases and insect pests.

break them down. By building humus, these soil denizens improve soil's physical and chemical properties as well as its biological health.

PROMOTING GOOD TILTH

Soil that has good physical qualities is said to be in good tilth. This means that it has good structure, and readily allows both air and water to enter and leave, while retaining enough of each to meet the needs of its inhabitants. It is easy to work using garden tools and presents little resistance to growing plant roots. Soil in good tilth resists erosion, holds water in time of drought, and holds enough air to prevent plants from drowning when it rains heavily. Although many people think first of plant nutrients when they think of soil fertility, tilth is at least as important—many fertility problems can be helped more by improving tilth than by adding fertilizers. Compost is the supreme soil conditioner, and will help improve structure that is either too light or too heavy.

Good soil structure is created by the formation of aggregates—irregularly shaped particles that stick together with lots of gaps and pore spaces between them. Soil with good structure will keep its shape after you squeeze it in your fist, but easily fall apart when you drop it. The gummy, spongy texture of humus is essential to forming aggregates and creating the crumb structure that establishes ideal conditions for biological activity. These aggregates hold air in the pore spaces, and each particle is covered with a thin film of water. Good soil structure means good drainage, as the spongy humus soaks up excess water and prevents roots from drowning, while water is able to drain out gradually through the pore spaces.

In dry times these pore spaces also serve a critical function by enabling moisture in lower levels of the soil to be wicked up to plant roots through a mechanism known as capillary action. Because humus can hold 80 to 90 percent of its own weight in water, it also serves as a reservoir that plants can use when they need it. It should come as no surprise that scientific research confirms that soil high in humus helps crops better withstand drought conditions.

Good structure also means good aeration, a necessity often overlooked in the quest for improved fertility. Most beneficial soil organisms, especially plant roots, need plenty of air to grow. This is one reason why cultivation often stimulates a flush of new plant growth, because more air is worked into the soil and more plant nutrients are released from organic matter—mineralized—as soil organisms grow faster. The same principle is at work when you turn your compost pile, making the organisms convert raw organic matter into humus more quickly.

After you apply compost, it breaks down further (mineralizes) over the following seasons. As soil organisms continue to dine on compost, it slowly releases its nutrients and helps make other soil nutrients available to plants—nutrients that would otherwise remain locked in soil aggregates.

In addition to improved air and water availability, the large amount of surface area of soil aggregates offers plenty of opportunities for the chemical interactions to take place that make nutrients available to soil organisms and to plants. So good soil structure provides an ideal habitat for soil organisms, with lots of places for them to live where they can get everything they need.

FERTILIZING SOIL—SLOWLY

Compost not only conditions soil but acts as a slow-release plant fertilizer. Calculations of nutrient values on fertilizer bags show only the amounts of soluble nitrogen, phosphorus and potassium immediately available to plants—and a bag of compost sold as fertilizer would have very small numbers on its label. But while it may be low in soluble nutrients, compost contributes in a major way to soil and plant nutrition as it is further broken down over time by soil organisms to release nutrients when plants need them. This slow release of nutrients has many advantages. Foremost is that while highly soluble fertilizers can easily dissolve in rainwater and wash away from the garden—threatening the health of nearby ground- and surface-water—the nutrients provided gradually by compost

A steady diet of compost will replenish and increase the microbial life in your soil, and keep your plants in the best of health.

are taken up by plants as they are released, and so are not wasted. If excessive amounts of nutrients are available to plants from highly soluble fertilizers, plants may take up more nutrients than they need; excess nitrogen in particular is undesirable because it creates lush, watery growth that is more susceptible to attack by pests and diseases. Aphids, for example, are attracted to plants with high levels of nitrogen in their leaves.

In addition to major plant nutrients, compost is rich in a well-balanced mix of micronutrients or trace elements, essential players in the molecular interactions on which all living organisms—including people—depend. While you can provide plants with other sources of these nutrients, the safest and most reliable way to provide them is through the compost pile. Plants need only tiny amounts of micronutrients, and too much of any of them can be harmful. Living tissue generally contains a good balance of micronutrients, so when it decomposes, its nutrients are made available in just the right proportions to feed new organisms.

Humus molecules bind these nutrients into chemical complexes in a process called *chelation*, which keeps them from washing away but makes them readily usable by plants and microbes. This same mechanism also helps detoxify soil if it is overdosed with essential nutrients, or even when it is contaminated with toxic heavy metals such as lead or cadmium.

Nutrients that plants need can also be stored efficiently on the large surface area of soil aggregates, chemically assisted by the colloids—gel-like substances—in humus. Positively charged nutrients, including calcium, magnesium,

Chemical fertilizers contain high levels of nitrogen, which creates lush, watery growth that is more susceptible to attack by diseases and insects, including aphids.

potassium and several important micronutrients, are held at these colloidal exchange sites, where they are available when plants need them, but will not be washed away.

Finally, we don't often think about the fact that carbon is really the most important food for plants, because they get most of it from the air in the form of carbon dioxide. However, humus is an important source of carbon for plants as well as for the organisms that consume its carbohydrates directly. As organic matter and humus decompose, carbon dioxide and other carbon-rich substances are released in the area near the soil surface, close to where plants are growing, and can significantly stimulate plant growth in this way alone.

UNLOCKING NUTRIENTS IN SOIL

Compost not only is rich in essential plant nutrients, but also helps stimulate the release of nutrients already present in soil but in unavailable forms. The availability of soil nutrients is strongly influenced by the soil's acidity, denoted as its pH. The ideal soil pH of 6.5 is slightly acid. Problems result when soil pH is either too low (acid) or too high (alkaline). Very acid soils can release excess micronutrients in harmful levels and lock up essential phosphorus. Alkaline soils have lots of minerals, but they are often locked up in chemically insoluble forms. Humus moderates both low and high pH, a quality known as buffering, and so improves the availability of nutrients in both acid and alkaline soils.

Compost also works biologically to improve nutrient availability. Its rich

Compost is now known to be a disease preventive. Compost tea, applied to plant leaves, staves off certain fungal diseases, including mildew.

diversity of microbes goes to work on rocks and decay-resistant organic materials, unlocking nutrients such as phosphorus for use by plants. Certain kinds of fungi, called mycorrhizae, actually form symbiotic relationships with plant roots, exchanging phosphorus extracted by the fungi from rock particles for carbohydrates produced by the plants.

FIGHTING PESTS & DISEASES

The value of compost goes beyond improving soil structure and providing nutrients. Soil health is, as we've seen, directly related to plant health. And, as is true of healthy people, healthy plants are better able to resist attack by pests and disease-causing pathogens. The right balance of nutrients, released at the rate at which they are needed by plants, helps prevent disease and insect problems, such as those caused by excess nitrogen. Compost also works directly to protect plants from soil-borne pathogens by inoculating them with organisms that fight disease. It is no accident that most antibiotics are derived from microorganisms that can be found in healthy soil. Compost tea, sprayed directly on crop leaves, has also been found to prevent certain fungal diseases such as mildew, and researchers are now able to produce custom composts that can suppress specific disease-causing organisms such as *Pythium,* a fungus that kills seeds and seedlings before or as they emerge from cool, wet soils (a widespread disease called damping-off).

In sum, compost is the ultimate all-around garden elixir. It won't work miracles, but a diet of compost will replenish and increase the life in your soil, and keep your plants in the best of health.

WHAT HAPPENS IN THE BIN

Compost Ecology

BY BENJAMIN GRANT

COMPOSTING IS THE ART OF managing an ongoing natural process for our own convenience and utility. This process, of course, is decomposition. In order to compost effectively, whatever the technique or motivation, it helps to understand decomposition. This process takes place whether we have a hand in it or not. It is the means by which organic material is returned to the soil for re-use and is accomplished by an astounding array of organisms known as decomposers, who together form a decomposer food chain, which depends entirely on dead organic material for energy.

THE CAST OF CHARACTERS

A visit to any backyard compost pile will yield a wide variety of visible decomposers. Earthworms of several types, sowbugs, millipedes, centipedes, mites, springtails and beetles abound in a healthy pile. Molds and other fungi, along with long, white strands of fungus-like actinomycetes, often sprout from the rotting material. The real action, however, is happening at the microscopic level. Billions of invisible bacteria, fungi and other

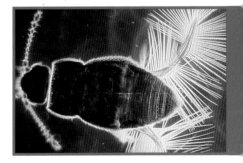

The feather-winged beetle feeds on the abundant fungal spores found in manure, compost and other rotting organics.

microorganisms consume the material in short order.

The members of this astonishingly diverse group of living things not only feed on the organic matter, they also interact with one another. Centipedes, for example, are predators, feeding on a variety of insects. Worms depend on bacteria to soften material up before they can consume it. As larger creatures break rotting matter apart, they expose more surface area and the microorganisms move in. All of this activity takes place in a moist medium, teeming with life, full of enzymes, sugars and nutrients, all of biological origin. In short, where there is decomposition, there is a complex ecosystem at work.

COMPOST METABOLISM

As in all ecosystems, the organisms in a compost pile thrive under certain specific conditions. This is where people come in. Successful composting is simply a matter of maintaining the appropriate habitat for the decomposers. Like mammals, the most desirable decomposers take in oxygen and use it to break down sugars for energy, releasing carbon dioxide and water. This is called aerobic metabolism, meaning "with oxygen."

Bacteria, being one-celled, cannot ingest complex materials, so much of their digestion must take place in the liquid medium that surrounds them. They accomplish this "extra-cellular" digestion by secreting the appropriate digestive enzymes into the solution, then taking up simple sugars as they become available. That's why a moist habitat is essential for bacteria.

Though decomposers depend on water, there can be too much of a good thing. A wet, mucky environment allows very little air to circulate, and anaerobic bacteria, which can decompose organic matter without oxygen, take over. These bacteria are much less efficient in the compost pile, and the by-products of their efforts can include ammonia, methane and alcohols—which smell awful. This process is better suited to swamps, where it occurs naturally, than to backyards, where it is quite avoidable.

Besides air and water, the ideal habitat for decomposers contains an appropriate balance of nutrients—most importantly carbon and nitrogen. Carbon is the energy source for the bacteria, and nitrogen is required to make proteins. Getting a good nutrient balance is simple (see "Developing a Sense of Humus," page 25).

If the balance of nutrients is just right, and water and air are abundant, bacterial activity really takes off. As aerobic bacteria consume sugars, they give off some of the energy as heat. With enough bacterial activity and a large enough pile, heat will start to accumulate and the temperature will rise, the same way it does when a person warms up with exercise. As the temperature in a compost pile rises, new heat-loving bacteria thrive. Temperatures in the best-managed "hot"—fast decomposing—backyard pile top out at around 130°F. But occasionally, in very large piles under ideal conditions, mesophilic (moderate-heat loving) and thermophilic (high-heat loving) bacteria can push the temperature above 150°F! (If temperatures go much higher, bacteria can die, so add air and water by turning the pile.) Many so-called cold, or passive piles never heat up significantly at all, and rot nicely anyway.

Some people want a lot of compost quickly and work hard to set up an ideal habitat for hot composting. Others prefer to approximate decomposition on the forest floor—cool, moist, and unhurried. The result is the same. In six weeks to two years, the decomposers will have broken the organic matter down into a rich, dark humus.

HUMUS AND THE SOIL

We tend to think of soil as dirt—inert, dull, lifeless. In reality, soil is a tremendously complex, fundamentally biological, substance. It is produced by and in turn allows the recycling of organic matter—the raw material of living things. The bulk of soil is rock weathered to various particle sizes,

The pseudoscorpion eats mites.

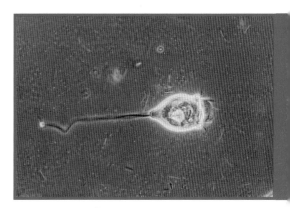

This protozoan feeds on organic detritus.

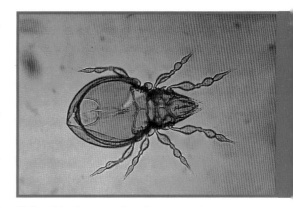

Oribatid mites are fungivorous—they eat mold—and nematodes. These mites are quite common members of the decomposer food web.

23

Slugs can wreak havoc in the garden but are benevolent in the compost pile.

Dont' be suprised if you find a wolf spider in your pile. They're there to eat smaller creatures such as mites.

especially sand, silt and clay. The remaining 1 to 5 percent is called the organic fraction of the soil, or humus, and consists of material that has been and will again be part of living organisms. But that's not the whole story. No soil is complete without water, air and enormous numbers of microorganisms, which give soil its characteristic chemical and ecological properties.

It has been estimated that there are more microorganisms in a teaspoon of compost than there are people on earth. By adding compost to the soil, you are adding billions of beneficial microorganisms. A complex, living soil is a healthier, more stable soil in which no one organism can erupt unchecked. We've grown accustomed to simplifying the equation with chemicals that do one job, but humus, like most things in the living world, serves a whole variety of functions, and is not easily replaced.

Decomposition is a spontaneous natural process, but if we understand it, we can nudge it in directions that suit us. Ask ten good gardeners the best way to compost, and you'll get ten different answers, but in each case the needs of the decomposers are looked after, and in each case the care is rewarded with rich, living soil.

DEVELOPING A SENSE OF HUMUS

Composting Basics

BY JOE KEYSER

THE KEY TO SUCCESSFUL COMPOSTING is getting started simply and properly, avoiding unwanted surprises and learning how to adjust your composting technique slowly to achieve a rich, beautiful product for your garden. Your compost pile will benefit hugely if you invest time and energy at the start, by building a proper free-standing or binned pile, by making sure that the materials you add are moist, by selecting a properly diverse assortment of materials for a compost "stew," and by periodically checking and correcting your pile's moisture content.

HOT, COLD OR WARM?

As you set out to build your pile, consider a few things. Do you need a lot of compost quickly for a new bed or garden area? Do you have roughly equal amounts of "browns" and "greens" (see chart on pages 34-35) on hand? Are there enough of these materials to build a sizeable pile—a cube about 3 feet on each side? Are you willing to chop your compostables into fine pieces and turn

Include a diverse assortment of ingredients in your "stew" so that the finished compost has a range of nutrients.

or aerate the pile thoroughly every three to seven days? If the answer to all of these questions is yes, think about building a hot, fast-working pile, where heat-loving bacteria quickly break down the organics. But if you answered no to any of these questions and would rather be planting than composting, consider slower, passive, cold composting. You will create finished compost—you'll just have to wait longer for it.

Keep in mind, too, that the end products of hot and cold composting are not equal. Recent research shows that hot compost is more likely to contain the microorganisms that give compost its disease-suppressing qualities. But hot compost loses more nitrogen during composting than is lost through cold composting. On the other hand, because a passive pile is exposed to the elements for long periods, it, too, loses nutrients. And because temperatures don't soar in a passive pile, weed seeds and pathogens can survive the process.

Site your pile on a level spot at least a foot away from any wooden structures.

Whether you decide you are a hot or a cold composter—or somewhere in the middle as is usually the case—you will find detailed directions on how to construct a range of pile types and other composting techniques on the following pages and in "From Pits to Piles," on page 40.

LOCATION

Site your compost pile on a level, easily accessible spot, near a water source if possible, and at least a foot away from any wooden structures—the fungi in your pile won't discriminate between twigs and your fence. Don't build bins or piles right up against a tree trunk or in a tree well—an invitation to bark-gnawing mice. The tree well will cut off air flow to the pile and to your tree's root system. Your pile will succeed equally well in either sun or shade, but gardeners in hot, dry climates often favor shaded spots where their compost is less likely to dry out. If you grow vegetables, set up your pile among the planting beds, so that the nutrients that leach out of it can enrich the soil and feed nearby plants. As a good neighbor policy, don't site your pile right on your property line or next to the neighbor's patio or window.

A pile that is covered won't get water-logged or leach valuable nutrients when there's lots of rain, snow or sleet.

WHY BIN?

You can compost by simply heaping organics on the ground or by piling them in a bin or other container. Composting bins come in a wide spectrum of designs and can allow you more control over the composting process, but they are often used primarily for aesthetic reasons. Among the other reasons to compost in bins: they can help organize materials and keep the garden tidy; they concentrate materials together in a smaller volume, and so encourage biological activity, which facilitates decomposition; and bins also help keep your materials moist and warm (bacteria give off heat as they metabolize). Bins also make sense for urban gardeners: if you make your bin rodent resistant with rodent screens or by using a metal trash can as your bin, you'll keep most pests out of your pile. And if you have a small garden, a bin will contain your compost in a neat, compact area. Make sure that the bin or bin system you choose can accommodate the volume of material you generate in your garden and kitchen.

Composters in predominantly wet climates may need to cover their bins, as high levels of precipitation can water-log a pile or allow valuable nutrients to leach away. If you live in a temperate climate, your bin will benefit from being open to the elements, as periodic rainfall can provide most of the moisture needed, especially if you make a concave- or funnel-shaped depression in the top of the pile to capture it. Cover the bin in cold, winter months, though, when biological activity slows, and additional moisture may only leach away nutrients. (See "Composting Coast to Coast," page 67, for more information on composting in different climates.)

Many composters prefer the laid-back approach; they let time and nature—especially earthworms—do most of the work. Make the most of this passive composting process by using two compost bins or systems, one for each alternating year. Fill one bin this year, the other next year and harvest from each every other year, back and forth, with a fraction of the turning, mixing and management. A two-bin system is also handy for hot composting; use one bin for the pile that's cooking, the other to collect ingredients for your next hot pile.

WHY NOT BIN?

Freestanding piles can work extremely well in most situations. If you want to create a hot, fast-working pile, you will need about one cubic yard (27 cubic feet) of material for adequate biomass to hold in heat and sustain a suitable metabolic process. If your pile is smaller than that, it will conserve moisture and heat inefficiently, and will work much more slowly, relying on invertebrates like worms, isopods (sowbugs and pillbugs) and millipedes to do much of the initial material decomposition. If you continue to add more and more material, your pile will reach the critical biomass and will become a faster working pile. Make sure that your pile or bin isn't taller than five feet; a pile that tall is not only awkward to manage, but the organic matter will become severely compacted and the circulation of oxygen in the pile reduced or cut off, which could result in sluggish, anaerobic conditions.

A GOOD BASE FOR A HOT PILE

If you are planning to run a quick, hot compost pile, before you throw the first handful of compostable material onto it, you must establish a good base. A 6- to 10-inch layer of brush is usually sufficient; form it by layering twigs, branches, corn stalks and other coarse material on the ground to form a crude mat, or break them up to fit inside a compost bin, if necessary. When you go to aerate the pile, don't bother turning the bottom 6 inches or so of the pile, as the brush layer will be difficult to turn. You can also use a wooden shipping pallet with half-inch spaces between slats as the base; pallets are plentiful and free and provide a smooth, flat surface on which pitchforks and other implements easily slide—and most commercial bins will sit right on top.

The compost base ensures all-important drainage for the pile. Materials left

By turning or aerating your pile, you increase the amount of air that gets to the oxygen-metabolizing microorganisms, speeding up decomposition.

directly on heavy, slow-to-drain ground can become saturated with water, resulting in an anaerobic—and malodorous—pile. If left in place too long, earth-hugging piles can also become infiltrated by tree roots, which will make harvesting the compost difficult—and potentially dangerous to the root system of the invading tree.

Raising the pile off the ground is the first, best step toward achieving a self- (also called passively) aerated hot pile, one that will need less turning and maintenance. The base allows an ample supply of oxygen to enter the pile *from the bottom*, one of the less widely known secrets of effective composting. Since the microorganisms in the pile generate heat and carbon dioxide as metabolic byproducts, the warm gas will rise and vent from the pile, creating an upward draft which will then draw fresh air into the pile naturally, from below—but only if the pile is sitting above the ground. Some composters advise interspersing perforated PVC pipes horizontally throughout the pile or vertically into the middle for ventilation, but I tested this method for eighteen months and noted no improvement.

TROUBLESHOOTING

Sometimes things go wrong—even with composting. Most composting problems stem from a lack of moisture, too much moisture, a nitrogen imbalance or poorly managed food scraps. Fortunately, all of these problems have a fairly simple solution. Below you will find a number of commonly encountered symptoms, their causes and their cures.

PROBLEM: Bad odor (like rotten eggs or spoiled food)
CAUSE: Uncovered or inappropriate food scraps
SOLUTION: Remove and discard any improper materials (meats, dairy, etc.); bury food scraps under a foot or more of inert materials.

PROBLEM: Bad odor (strong ammonia, rotting seaweed, pond scum, swamp gas)
CAUSE: Anaerobic pile

SOLUTION: Turn materials, mixing in dry leaves, straw or wood chips. Check base of pile for proper drainage.

PROBLEM: Bad odor (strong ammonia, moldy hay)
CAUSE: Too much grass
SOLUTION: Mix grass with other dry or high-carbon materials or remove some grass, spread out to dry and mix back into pile.

PROBLEM: Insect pests
CAUSE: This is not necessarily a problem
SOLUTION: Not all insects in a compost pile are "pests"; the compost ecosystem includes a host of useful invertebrates, including millipedes, centipedes, worms, ants—even snails and slugs, among others.

PROBLEM: Insect pests
CAUSE: Too dry, not mixed properly
SOLUTION: Make sure food materials are properly buried, and turn the

COMPOSTABLE MATERIALS

Homes and gardens across the country produce a wide variety of organic materials in very different proportions. Yard trimmings—leaves, grass, weeds, brush and prunings—make up the major share of compostables, although kitchen scraps and agricultural manures can also play a significant role. And

outer layer of materials into core of pile. Hot piles will destroy or deter most insects, such as grubs and other larvae (maggots). Moisten pile if necessary; moist piles deter bees and wasps. Wood chips and woody material taken from rotted wood piles or municipal mulch piles may contain termites and/or carpenter ants.

PROBLEM: Animal pests
CAUSE: Improper food handling
SOLUTION: Most animals will be deterred if you bury food under other materials; for persistent problems, especially with rodents, stop adding food, use an enclosed bin, or change bin design to restrict access. A secure lid will discourage most possums, raccoons, and birds.

PROBLEM: Pile not breaking down
CAUSE: Insufficient nitrogen
SOLUTION: Add grass, manure, kitchen scraps or other natural nitrogen sources.

PROBLEM: Pile not breaking down
CAUSE: Pile is too dry
SOLUTION: Add water while turning until pile is moist, but not wet; should feel like a sponge throughout.

PROBLEM: Pile not breaking down
CAUSE: Poor aeration
SOLUTION: Start turning and mixing materials more often; check integrity of base, replace if broken down.

PROBLEM: Pile heats up, then stops
CAUSE: Poor aeration
SOLUTION: Hot piles need lots of fresh oxygen; turn materials as pile starts to cool down. It might be necessary to add an additional nitrogen source periodically.

PROBLEM: Pile is slightly warm at middle
CAUSE: Pile is too small
SOLUTION: Binned piles require a minimum of about 18 to 20 cubic feet to work efficiently. Add more materials if possible, or use a smaller bin to concentrate the pile's volume.

while almost anything organic will decompose, it does not mean that everything should simply be tossed into a compost bin and forgotten.

Leaves Leaves are generally the easiest materials to manage and are frequently the carbon-rich backbone of most piles in temperate areas. All leaves can be composted, from *Abelia* to *Zelkova* and all the ash, maples and oaks in-between.

Fall leaves are rich in carbon.

Grass gives compost a shot of nitrogen.

Leaves can be composted whole, or shredded and gathered up with a lawn mower and bagging attachment, or chopped up with a dedicated power shredder. As is the case with all compostable materials, reducing particle size will accelerate the decomposition process. When you add leaves to a pile or bin, moisten *as you add them*. It's almost impossible to add water to leaf pile after the fact—it's just shed off the top. Place a few armfuls into the bin and use a hose with spray attachment to thoroughly moisten them; repeat the process, adding water at each step.

Leaves can be composted all by themselves, producing a humus-rich leaf-mold in about one year, if the pile is turned several times per season. Or the process can be hastened by incorporating other nitrogen-rich materials, like grass clippings and weeds, into the mix, producing a finer, loam-like compost.

Grass Grass clippings are the second most widely composted yard material. They're full of nitrogen, and can speed up the decomposition of carbonaceous materials such as leaves, straw or chipped brush. Most savvy gardeners realize that healthy lawns thrive when clippings are "grasscycled," or left on the lawn after mowing. However, if the grass has grown taller than four inches, perhaps due to a vigorous growth spurt in early spring or after a long rainy spell, it might be beneficial to remove the clippings from the lawn to avoid creating a heavy blanket of clumps and to add them to the compost pile. You might also remove grass clippings from time to time as a special snack for the pile's protein-hungry bacteria or perhaps to jump-start a sluggish pile.

Grass should never be composted by itself—in fact, most odor complaints about compost piles result from piles made up of clippings alone. Grass is over 90 percent water and the thin blades rapidly clump together, forming anaerobic masses that give off a strong ammonia odor. Always mix grass thoroughly into other dry or higher-carbon materials. Don't put grass onto the pile in thick layers, and don't just dump loads of grass onto a working pile. Always work grass well into a pile.

Food scraps Spoiled vegetables, fruits and kitchen scraps provide a rich, free source of nitrogen. Coffee grounds contain as much nitrogen as grass clippings, and can even be brought home by the bucket from gourmet coffee shops. Tea leaves and tea bags, coffee filters, corn husks and cobs, fruit rinds, vegetable trimmings, egg shells and a plethora of peels and scrapings are prime candidates for the pile. But *do not add* meat and dairy-related products which have a dense, high-protein composition that is likely to attract anaerobic bacteria, and to result in sulfide gases and other odors of putrefaction. Various undesirable

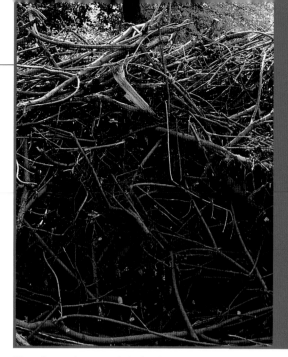
Shred woody materials for hot compost.

Kitchen scraps are great compostables.

insects are also likely to breed on the pile, leaving behind larvae (maggots). And it will also attract larger, four-legged pests.

Bury all food items, including spoiled fruits taken directly from the garden, at least one foot into an existing pile. If you drop scraps onto the top of the pile, even in an enclosed bin, you are guaranteed to attract fruit flies, gnats, maggots and larger "winged" and "tailed" pests. In urban areas or communities with rodent problems, a completely enclosed unit, such as a lidded metal trash can with small holes or an indoor worm box, should be used.

Weeds Even the best gardeners have to pull weeds, but it is the wise com-

COMMON COMPOSTABLES

B R O W N S (carbon-rich, dry)

Fall leaves and plants	Don't add any material from plants that are diseased
Straw or hay	Watch for hay seeds; if they get in the pile they may survive the composting process
Pine needles	These are covered with a waxy coating and may take a while to break down
Twigs	If these are larger than the circumference of your thumb, chop them into smaller pieces
Newspaper	Best recycled, but can boost carbon content in pile; tear into small shreds and add in thin layers
Eggshells	These are an excellent addition to the pile because of their high calcium content; crush before adding
Wood chips	Make sure to provide a good nitrogen source to balance the heavy carbon content in the chips
Corncobs	Chop into small pieces with pruners or a knife
Fireplace ashes	Ash is a good source of potassium for the pile but add sparingly; never add ash from charcoal briquets
Sawdust	Like wood chips, a good source of carbon; make sure that your sawdust is not from pressure-treated wood

posting gardener who turns weeds into a success story. Weeds are like grass, succulent and full of nitrogen, and should be cheerfully mixed into the pile. But *don't* add to the pile invasive weeds such as morning glories, weeds with vigorous rhizomes such as quackgrass, or weeds that have already set seed, all of which can use the rich compost as a jumping off spot for other inviting areas in the garden.

COMMON COMPOSTABLES

GREENS (nitrogen-rich, wet)

Fresh leaves or plants . . . . .Just put them in; they'll rot

Kitchen scraps . . . . .Add peelings and waste from vegetables and fruits; chop tough peels such as citrus

Coffee grounds, tea bags . . .Excellent for the pile because readily available and high in nitrogen; filters are okay, too

Green grass . . . . .Mix thoroughly with other ingredients, or you may have anaerobic layers

Weeds . . . . .Try to get these into the pile before they set seed and omit pernicious plants like bindweed and quackgrass

Seaweed . . . . .Add only small amounts because can contain high levels of salts

Flowers . . . . .Add deadheads and freshly trimmed blooms

Freshly pruned trimmings .If prunings are woody, chop them into smaller pieces

Manure and bedding . . . . .Add manure from farm animals and small pets; these will really heat up your pile. Don't add cat or dog droppings.

Brown, carbonaceous materials give the compost pile mass and enhance aeration while green, nitrogenous organics encourage microorganisms to reproduce. Add browns and greens to your pile in about equal amounts, and mix thoroughly as you build the pile. Sooner or later you'll harvest a nutritious finished compost and superb soil conditioner for your garden.

Woody materials Hedge trimmings, small twigs and branches, stalks, wood mulch (both old and new), pine cones, large seed pods and other woody matter and brush are extremely high in carbon and will take longer to decompose than leaves. You can speed up their decomposition by chipping larger woody pieces, or at least cutting them up with lopping shears or hand pruners. A good rule of thumb is never to add anything longer than six inches in length or thicker than

Add green trimmings to the pile.

Seaweeds are rich in micronutrients.

Animal manure is a valuable ingredient.

half an inch. Larger materials will simply haunt the compost pile for years to come and make turning the pile more difficult. If you have access to a chipper, turn these large pieces into a mulch for the garden.

Other trimmings Ornamental grasses, decorative vines, dead-headed flowers, annuals, perennial prunings and most of the other herbaceous material in the garden can and should be added to the pile. As with woody materials, chop up these materials into pieces as small as possible. Pine needles can be also be added, although they are somewhat slow to break down and can always be used immediately as a mulch wherever you grow acid-loving plants.

Agricultural manures Animal manures are a wonderful source of nitrogen and other nutrients, especially for gardeners without access to grass clippings. Poultry manure is a concentrated source of nitrogen, although the odor is rather difficult to work around. Cow manure is one of the most valuable additions to the compost pile and the garden, while horse manure may be more readily available from stables, even in most urban areas. Keep in mind that agricultural manures, especially stable "sweepings," often harbor viable hay seeds. If you can maintain a hot compost pile—130°-160°F—for several days successively, you will destroy most of the remaining seeds.

Keep pesticide-treated plants and pressure-treated wood scraps and sawdust, which contain copper, cyanide and arsenic, out of your compost.

Household materials Compostable materials from around the house are usually carbon-rich, including black and white newspaper sections (almost every newspaper is now printed with soy-based inks), corrugated and uncoated cardboard, dried flowers, wood or fireplace ash (never charcoal or coal ash), and untreated sawdust. Cardboard and newspaper should be ripped-up into strips and moistened, preferably by soaking in a bucket of water.

MATERIALS TO AVOID

Good hygiene is as important for keeping the compost pile healthy as it is for overall garden health. Don't add diseased plant materials to your compost pile because viruses and other pathogens, including nematodes and related pests, are not always destroyed in the composting process. Abide by the adage, "when in doubt, throw it out."

Chemical manufacturers may say otherwise, but it is advisable to keep pesticide-treated plants, including grass clippings, out of your compost, especially if the finished product is to be used in a vegetable garden. The same goes for pressure-treated wood scraps and sawdust, which contain copper, cyanide and arsenic.

Do not add irritating plant materials such as poison sumac and poison ivy, as the oils in these plants, urushiol, will not break down, although nettles will break down completely.

Avoid adding any food materials which have been mixed with shortenings, spreads, meats or dairy products for the reason cited above; fats and oils coating other organic materials will inhibit their contact with oxygen, slowing down decomposition. Never add bones, fat or meat itself, because as explained earlier, they will attract pests and create odors.

Add grain-derived foods with caution because these contain sugars, fats and oils among other substances, which may attract pests. And never add the fecal waste of dogs, cats or other carnivorous pets, which may expose you to disease pathogens both when handling and using the compost.

Three stages in the life of a compost pile: above, uncomposted compostables; opposite left, the middle stage of decomposition, and opposite right, finished compost.

While not dangerous, some other items are best left out of the pile as well, including the waxy leaves of magnolias and hollies, which break down very slowly, pine cones and sweet gum "balls," among other stubborn materials—unless they are first chipped to speed them on their way.

DO NOT ADD

Charcoal or coal ash
Meat or dairy-related materials
   or shortenings
Bones, fat or meat
Pet droppings
Pesticide-treated plants and
   grass clippings
Pressure-treated wood scraps
   and sawdust
Poison sumac and poison ivy
Grain-derived foods

THE RIGHT STUFF

The kinds of materials you include, how well you construct the pile and how you manage it over time, will determine the quality of the final compost product. For best results, a compost pile must be, as the word implies, a composite of different materials.

Most composting literature revolves around the legendary and ideal carbon-to-nitrogen (C:N) ratio of 30:1, both components in all organic matter. The various strains of bacteria that are primarily responsible for decomposi-

tion have an ideal "diet" of 30:1, where the carbohydrates in the carbon-rich matter are balanced by a suitable proportion of protein or nitrogen. Most deciduous leaves have a C:N range of 50-70:1, while grass clippings, manures and food scraps have a range of 15-20:1; woody materials often range as high as 500:1. Too much nitrogen in a pile results in the formation of ammonia gas; too much carbon and the pile will sulk for years. Mix the ingredients together, and a balance is achieved, resulting in a C:N more ideal for the bacteria—and therefore a faster, harder-working compost pile.

Getting to the ideal mix of materials is generally a process of experimentation, of mixing different types of material when they become seasonably available. In autumn and winter, gather fallen leaves and put them in the bin; in spring and summer, collect grass and other green plant matter and mix them into the pile. As you blend the materials, the temperature of the pile will rise, signifying a dramatic increase in biological activity. In general, try to combine at least equal parts of nitrogen-rich (green, wet) material with high carbon (brown, dry) material (see page 34). A long-favored composting recipe that will work in most yards is to mix equal parts of grass and leaves; this stew is sure to heat up within a day or two and to shrink in volume by 50 percent in less than a week.

During spring and summer, or when outdoor temperatures climb into the fifties and above, and when green matter is readily available, turn or aerate the pile every time you add new materials. Mix and aerate hot, fast-working piles—those that make pitchfork tines hot to the touch when thrust in the middle or that "steam" as you poke into it—every two weeks or so. Thoroughly blend together every bit of organic material, especially from the cooler sides and top of the pile. If you turn it less often, you will also get a good compost product, but it will take longer.

FROM PITS TO PILES

Composting Techniques

BY PATRICIA JASAITIS

LONG BEFORE I LEARNED how to compost, I understood the rewards of recycling in the garden. During her daily trips to the citrus trees, slop bucket and shovel in hand, my grandmother shared an important lesson with me: "Return to the earth what she produces." She buried the rinds right back into the soil around the fruitful trees in return for their favor of bearing our breakfast.

As my grandmother did, you can improve the soil in your garden without actually constructing a compost pile. After all, the act of making a compost pile isn't what enriches the soil; it's the subsequent spreading of the finished compost. In fact, you can add organic matter to the earth in two forms, as raw material or as already composted, rotted matter.

To come up with a plan for recycling your organic waste, examine the different materials that come from your yard and your kitchen. Decide how much energy, time and space you are willing to contribute to their decomposition. You may decide on a strategy that includes a few different techniques or a single approach. Among the options are alternative techniques such as my grandmother's pit composting method or composting in a typical pile.

MULCH AND COMPOST ON THE SPOT

If traditional composting seems like too much work—loading a bin, maintain-

The act of making a compost pile isn't what enriches the soil; it's the subsequent spreading of the finished compost.

Pit composting is useful for food scraps or garden trimmings.

Layer garden materials and food scraps in your compost trench.

ing the compost and, when done, unloading it and spreading it—consider the following options. Using all of these methods, you can add organic matter right where it will best benefit the soil.

Pit composting Pit composting is a useful method when you have a batch of food scraps or garden trimmings to dispose of. Pick places for pits around the garden—either at random, in an organized circuit or concentrated in an area that most needs soil improvement. Using a shovel or post-hole digger, dig however many holes you need 8- to 12-inches deep, dump in the donations and cover back up with soil. Be careful not to re-open a recently filled pit; food can decay anaerobically when underground and smell sour. Within six months to a year, the decomposition should be complete and you can plant the area. If rodents, raccoons and even bigger scavengers are a concern, you may want to consider another method of food composting.

Trench composting Like pit composting, trench composting is a method of burying raw material in the garden. Dig a trench any length, 1 to 3 feet wide by 12 to 18 inches deep, spreading the dug-up soil next to the trench. Over time, layer garden materials and food scraps, making sure to bury or cover food scraps beneath a thick layer of leaves or something less putrescible than food. When the trench is close to full, top it with the removed soil and open up another. Vegetable gardens and flower beds are good candidates for trench composting.

Digester composting Putting kitchen-scraps in a digester is one type of pit composting that won't have you constantly working with the shovel. Commercial digester units are available and look like cone-shaped garbage cans, which you partially sink into the ground. You can also make your own digester by sinking a garbage can at least halfway into the soil. Punch holes in the underground portion of the container to allow the food's moisture to drain out while allowing microorganisms and worms to get in. Digesters won't provide you with lots of finished compost—most of it just shrinks away and may disappear into the soil. Empty out the finished compost after six months or so and move the digester occasionally to enrich the soil in more than one area.

Most of the organics you put in a digester disappear into the soil.

Sheet composting Spread a batch of leaves, manure or other organics onto the soil and mix it in with a fork or rototiller; this is sheet composting. You can apply a layer up to 8 inches thick. Let a few months pass, during which the materials will decay, before planting. During the off-season, sheet-compost dormant vegetable and annual flower beds; this will do a lot to improve the soil, and the beds will be ready to plant in spring.

Green manuring is a great way to add lots of organics to your soil.

Green manure By green manuring—growing a crop and then turning it under into the earth—you can add large amounts of organic matter to the soil. Good candidate crops for green manure include rye, buckwheat or clover, to

Mulching mowers cut and chop grass into fine pieces that fall back to the ground, returning organic matter to the soil that generated it.

name just a few. The plant matter will decompose quickly—within a month or so because it is still young, soft and full of nitrogen. Plant in the fall to cover the soil over the winter, then till the cover crop under before planting in the spring. Or if you have extra space in your garden, plant a cover crop in the spring and let it grow for a full year; the soil that you turn this crop into will be *much* improved.

"Grass-cycling" You don't have to bag or rake grass clippings—just let them fall into the lawn. When you "grass mulch," you return organic matter right back to the soil that generated it. Mulching mowers and mulching kits for regular mowers effectively cut and chop grass into fine pieces. Regular mowers can mulch mow, too, if the blades are kept very sharp and you cut only a third of the height of your lawn each time.

In the spring, when growing grass can be heavy and wet, gather the clippings to use as mulch or for compost-pile fodder. You may also want to collect grass clippings as fuel for a hot compost pile.

In fall, in all but the heaviest weeks of leaf drop, mow leaves right into the grass—another easy way to take care of cleanup. Cemeteries, parks and golf courses do this to save time and energy, and keep soil and turf in good shape.

Mulching The simplest way to add organic materials is to mulch on top of soil. The blanket of mulch will break down very slowly and disappear in a few years. Until then it will protect the soil from erosion, reduce the number of weeds and keep the soil moist and insulated. Gather leaves as they fall and pile them under trees, shrubs or on flower beds, 1 to 3 inches deep. Lay twigs, branches and hedge trimmings right on the ground, especially in inconspicuous spots. To turn these into more presentable, refined mulches, run over leaves or twigs with a mower, feed them into a chipper/shredder or shred leaves with a vacuum-blower. If you don't own any of these machines, get out your gloves and hand pruners and chop these woody materials by hand; this will do the trick— and can be therapeutic, too.

SLOW OR FAST COMPOSTING?

Some people who compost like to brag about their hot, fast piles with steamy tales—"I can make finished compost in *14 days*." But with a minimum of work, a cold, slow, passive pile will produce finished compost in anywhere from a few months to a few years. The amount of time, physical energy and attention required for hot, fast, active composting is much greater, and you trade off your energy for faster decomposition—usually two to three months. Fast composting is an impressive process, but passive composting is all the more amazing as it requires so little work.

Hot composting will usually kill off weed seeds and disease organisms, while slow compost may boast a higher nitrogen content in the finished product.

Perhaps the most important thing to remember about a slow-to-rot pile versus a hot one is that you can gradually add materials to a slow pile but to create a hot pile in a large bin, you must put together all the materials all at once—or within a few weeks, or less. Decide whether you have the volume of materials—one cubic yard of organics—or the will to import ingredients to supplement your own.

If you're planning a slow-to-rot pile, you can gradually add materials, then sit back and relax while they compost.

SLOW AND EASY

All organic matter will rot no matter what you do or don't do to it. For slow and easy compost, just pile materials up as they become available. (Slow piles are sometimes called cold even though temperatures might climb above 100°F, since the peak temperature isn't as high as in a fast pile and doesn't last as long.) A big heap is the lowest-maintenance type of slow compost pile. You can situate it in a spot that's out of the way so that you don't have to see the pile all the time and don't have to work it often if at all. You may harvest finished compost, if you ever do, many years later and from the bottom of the pile.

You can also let bins full of leaves rot very slowly without a fuss, and you can use the resulting leaf compost or "leaf mold" at many stages of decomposition, from coarse and flaky with bits of leaves intact to very fine particles. Sod can also be composted in a cool pile: stack sod pieces upside down, and water and cover with a tarp. This heap will rot slowly, finishing in one to two years.

A slightly more involved method of slow composting requires a bit more work: you will need to do some preparation before putting the materials onto the pile. Include a mix of brown and green materials to make the pile go faster than one that's mostly dry and brown. Chop woody or long materials to keep the pile easy to turn and to open up spots to bury food scraps. Sprinkle water onto the pile as you add materials, and turn as often or as infrequently as you choose. The payback for your work is a slightly speedier, more easily harvested compost.

Here are three different ways to manage and harvest cold piles, and the bins that work for each method.

Single pile   A single pile is the least space-demanding way to contain all stages of compost, old and new. When you turn this pile, you may blend fresh ingredients with older materials, so to harvest compost, you will probably have to separate the finished from the unfinished. Tear apart the pile or fish near the bottom for the finished compost, returning any raw materials back to give them more time to decay.

For this method, you'll need to either put together a free-standing heap without enclosures, or purchase one of the following to contain your pile: a holding bin such as a commercial plastic bin, chicken-wire cylinder, garbage can, homemade wood or brick bin with solid, fixed walls, or a tumbler.

Single bin with bottom access   A single bin holds all material layered in different stages of decay, with the oldest materials at the bottom and the newest kept at the top. At the bottom of the bin, a removable door or panel permits

RECYCLING OPTIONS FOR YARD TRIMMINGS AND KITCHEN SCRAPS

All of the following materials can be thrown onto the compost pile (or buried in the middle in the case of food scraps) or returned to the soil through one of the options outlined below.

GRASS CLIPPINGS

1) Leave on the lawn. NOTES: Cut off only ⅓ of grass height at a time using regular or mulching mower.

2) Mulch. NOTES: Use around trees, shrubs, on flower or vegetable beds. Apply 1" thick.

LEAVES

1) Mow and leave on lawn. NOTES: Mow with regular or mulching mower in all but heaviest leaf fall.

2) Mulch. NOTES: Apply a 1"-3" thick layer, either whole or shredded with bag mower, vacuum-blower or chipper/shredder.

3) Sheet, trench or pit compost. NOTES: Dig into or till under soil.

WOODY PRUNINGS, BRANCHES, TWIGS, HEDGE CLIPPINGS, DEAD PLANTS, CHRISTMAS TREES AND GREENS

1) Mulch. NOTES: Chop or shred for the neatest mulch, or layer larger pieces for an informal look.

FRESH TRIMMINGS, WEEDS, SPENT PLANTS, OLD POTTING SOIL

1) Sheet, pit or trench compost. NOTES: Bury small amounts at a time or till a larger batch into the soil.

SOD

1) Sod pile. NOTES: Stack upside down in pile and cover with tarp for 1-2 years.

FOOD SCRAPS

1) Pit or trench compost. NOTES: Make sure to cover with 8"-12" of soil.

2) Digester. NOTES: Buy unit or sink garbage can in ground.

3) Indoor or outdoor worm compost. NOTES: Add worms to regular compost pile or keep a separate bin (see "Let Worms Do Your Work," page 73).

access to the oldest, most decayed compost. You will need to either make a wood, wire or brick bin with removable bottom slats or purchase a commercial plastic or wood bin with a bottom door to hold the pile.

Cold composting in batches Keep at least two bins running at once, one for "receiving," another for "cooking." Load materials into only one bin at a time. When full, stop adding to that bin, let it rot into a batch of finished material and open up a second bin for any new materials to compost.

You will need any two or more bins listed above, with or without easy bottom access, or a tumbler and another bin or two tumblers, so that you can alternate cooking and receiving batches.

SPEEDY AND STEAMY

When the conditions in your compost pile are just right, the resident bacteria go into a feeding frenzy and give off a lot of heat, which makes the compost "hot." If a fast turn-around time is important to you and you have enough materials to load up one cubic yard within a week or two, consider hot composting. Smaller piles may not be able to trap the heat, but you can keep them warmer by insulating the pile with hay bales, bubble wrap or foam insulation panels. These insulators also effectively trap compost heat in cold weather.

For your compost to get really hot, you'll need to:
- make sure the pile is large enough
- add a lot of nitrogen-rich, green ingredients
- shred large and tough materials
- keep the moisture content right, and
- aerate the pile by turning and mixing about once a week or by aerating passively with perforated pipes.

You can keep burying food scraps into the middle of a hot compost pile during the first two-thirds of the process—any later and the food may not be decayed when the rest of the pile is ready to harvest. Here are two ways to run and harvest hot piles, both in batches.

Single bin Load your bin all at once or at the most over the course of a few weeks. Then stop adding materials, and let your pile decompose as one batch of compost, turning it completely every three to seven days. Pile new organic debris in a waiting area for your next hot pile in a holding bin or free-standing heap. Store food scraps in the refrigerator or layer them in a bucket with dry garden materials in the meantime until you can get a new active batch going.

You will need either a commercial wood or wire holding bin, 1-cubic-yard capacity, preferably with easy to open front slats or door for turning; or a homemade wood, wire or brick bin, 1-cubic-yard capacity, with removable front slats; or a large-capacity tumbler. You will also need an extra holding bin for storing materials before processing.

Multiple-bins Using a series of bins lined up next to each other, you can keep a few batches of compost active, loading one bin until full, then filling the next one. Move and turn the compost down the line, from one bin to the next, to provide aeration and mixing and to permit the older piles to finish cooking while the newest, hottest pile is getting started.

You will need one of the following: two or more commercial wood or wire bins connected to a turning unit with good front access; a homemade wood, wire or brick turning unit of two or more connected bins; any two or more free-standing holding bins (choose bins with front access, which make turning the compost easier); or a large tumbler plus at least one other bin; start batch in tumbler and then turn into extra bin.

To succeed at hot composting, you'll need to monitor the moisture in the pile.

Bury kitchen scraps in a hot pile early in the "cooking" process.

WORMS AT WORK

Worms are an essential denizen in compost piles indoors (see "Let Worms Do Your Work, page 73) and out. Although some garden-variety worms may show up on their own in the lowest layers of your backyard compost pile, you can boost the worm population by adding a special kind of worm—redworms (also known as red wigglers and brandling worms)—which are especially well suited

You can boost the worm population in your compost pile by adding a special kind of worm—redworms. You may want to add them to slow, cold compost piles and let them "turn" the compost for you, speeding up the rate of decomposition.

to moving through and devouring a compost heap.

Redworms prefer fresh organic matter to garden soil and do best in temperatures from 50° to 80° degrees. Each worm can consume up to its own weight every day—imagine if humans did that! Organic matter eventually passes through the worms' bodies several times, so worm compost (called "castings") is extra-rich in nitrogen compared to regular compost, and can be used as a fertilizer.

Redworms are really useful in slow, cold compost piles. Because they move around throughout the heap, the worms "turn" the compost for you and speed up the rate of decomposition. Don't expect worms to stay in the middle of a hot pile; they will search for cooler quarters temporarily, and when the core cools, the worms will return to finish off the feast. If your pile will ever be subject to extreme cold or heat, make sure that the bin has an opening to the ground, so the worms can move into the soil if necessary.

BUILD YOUR OWN BIN—OR BENCH

A-Z Plans for Two Composters

BY PATRICIA JASAITIS & JEFF WILKINSON

HERE ARE PLANS FOR TWO HANDSOME BINS that you can build yourself. We've included detailed drawings, a list of materials needed for each bin and a brief description that will guide you through the assembly process. Both bins have removable slats in the front, and in the two-bin system, between the bins as well. Slide the slats out and you should have no problem turning your pile. For extra comfort, the compost bench has a back and arms, but these can be left out to simplify construction.

If possible, choose rot-resistant woods such as cedar or salvaged redwood. You can also use pine, which is less expensive but also less rot resistant, and just replace parts of your bin as they go. Do not use pressure-treated woods for these bins, because they have been treated with heavy metals such as arsenic, which can leach out into your compost and from there into your garden.

Many lumber yards sell lumber "cut to size," and will sell you the specific pieces you need if you provide them with a list (see pages 52 and 54). They will probably not cut the curves and angles that are part of the arms and back of the compost bench, so you will need a jigsaw to cut those. You'll also need a drill to pre-drill screw holes where thin pieces join or near the edge of boards, to avoid splitting the wood. Other tools that will come in handy include an electric screwdriver, hammer, wrench and level, and for the compost bench you'll also need a steel square, hand saw and chisel.

Novice carpenters will find the two-bin composter easier to assemble than the bench as it has fewer parts and no curved or angled pieces. If possible, put this

continues on page 56

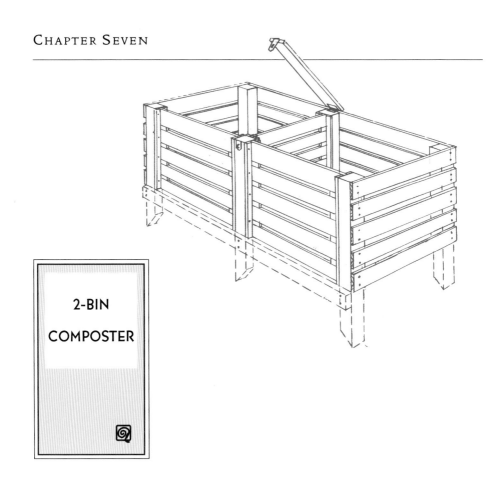

2-BIN

COMPOSTER

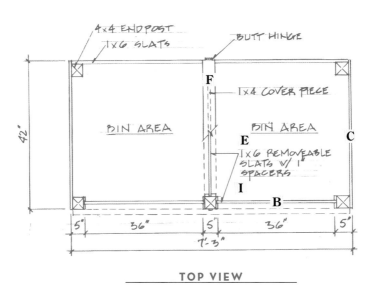

4x4 END POST
1x6 SLATS
BUTT HINGE

F
1x4 COVER PIECE

BIN AREA   BIN AREA   C

E

1x6 REMOVEABLE
SLATS W/ 1"
SPACERS

I

B

42"

5"   36"   5"   36"   5"

7'-3"

TOP VIEW

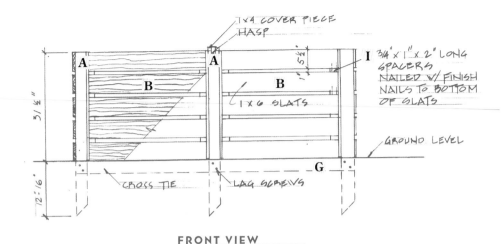

1x4 COVER PIECE
HASP
3/4" x 1" x 2" LONG
SPACERS
NAILED W/ FINISH
NAILS TO BOTTOM
OF SLATS

1x6 SLATS
GROUND LEVEL
CROSS TIE
LAG SCREWS

FRONT VIEW

MATERIALS LIST FOR 2-BIN COMPOSTER

Wood:
A: 6 posts 3½" x 3½" x 47½"
B: 10 slats ¾" x 5½" x 35¾"
C: 10 slats ¾" x 5½" x 42"
D: 5 slats ¾" x 5½" x 7' 1½"
E: 5 slats ¾" x 5½" x 34¾"
F: 1 cover piece ¾" x 3½" x 42"
G: 1 cross tie 1½" x 3½" x 7' 3"
H: 12 stops ¾" x 1¼" x 31½"
I: 24 spacers ¾" x 1" x 2"

Hardware:
hasp: heavy-duty hasp, 7½"
 long, galvanized finish
hinge: 3" x 3" brass, butt hinge
screws: 110 1½" x No. 10
 stainless, flat-head self-
 driving screws
lag screws: six 3" x ½"
 diameter
nails: 40 galvanized finish nails

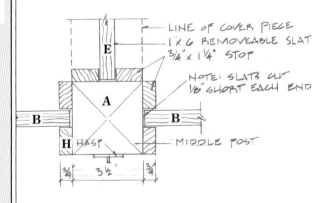

LINE OF COVER PIECE
1X6 REMOVEABLE SLAT
¾" x 1¼" STOP

NOTE: SLATS CUT
1/8" SHORT EACH END

MIDDLE POST
HASP

DETAIL OF MID-POST

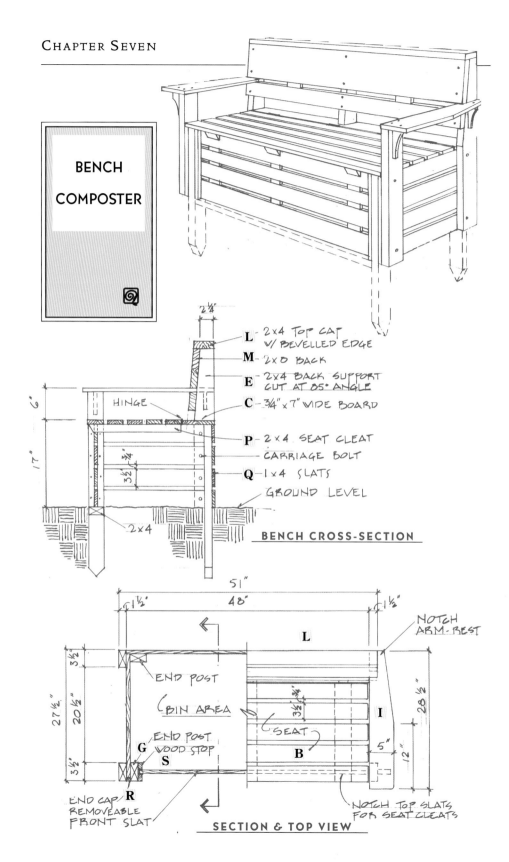

BENCH

COMPOSTER

L - 2x4 TOP CAP W/ BEVELLED EDGE

M - 2x0 BACK

E - 2x4 BACK SUPPORT CUT AT 05° ANGLE

C - 3/4" x 7" WIDE BOARD

HINGE

P - 2x4 SEAT CLEAT

- CARRIAGE BOLT

Q - 1x4 SLATS

- GROUND LEVEL

2x4

2 1/8"

6"

17"

3 1/2"

3/4"

BENCH CROSS-SECTION

51"

48"

1 1/2"

1 1/2"

L

NOTCH ARM-REST

3 1/2"

END POST

20 1/2"

27 1/2"

BIN AREA

3 1/2"

3/4"

I

28 1/2"

SEAT

END POST WOOD STOP

G

S

B

5"

12"

END CAP REMOVEABLE FRONT SLAT

R

NOTCH TOP SLATS FOR SEAT CLEATS

SECTION & TOP VIEW

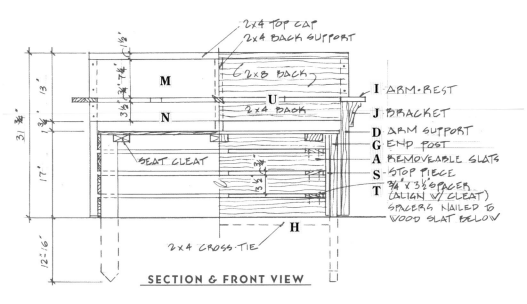

2x4 TOP CAP
2x4 BACK SUPPORT
2x8 BACK
M
U
N
2x4 BACK
I ARM·REST
J BRACKET
D ARM SUPPORT
G END POST
A REMOVEABLE SLATS
S STOP PIECE
T ¾" X 3½" SPACER (ALIGN W/ CLEAT)
SPACERS NAILED TO WOOD SLAT BELOW
SEAT CLEAT
2x4 CROSS·TIE

SECTION & FRONT VIEW

MATERIALS LIST
FOR COMPOST BENCH

Wood:

A: 4 front slats ¾" x 3½" x 44¾"

B: 5 seat slats ¾" x 3½" x 47¾"

C: 1 back seat slat ¾" x 7" x 48"

D: 2 front arm supports
1½" x 3½" x 22¼"

E: 2 back supports
1½" x 3½" x 30¼"

F: 1 middle back support
1½" x 3½" x 13¼"

G: 4 end posts 1½" x 3½" x 32¼"

H: 1 crosstie 1½" x 3½" x 45"

I: 2 arm rests ¾" x 5" x 28½"

J: 2 front brackets ¾" x 2½" x 5"

K: 2 back brackets ¾" x 2" x 4½"

L: 1 top cap 1½" x 3½" x 51"

M: 1 back 1½" x 7¼" x 51"

N: 1 back 1½" x 3½" x 51"

O: 8 side slats ¾" x 3½" x 26"

P: 3 seat cleats 1½" x 3½" x 19"

Q: 4 back slats ¾" x 3½" x 48"

R: 2 end caps ¾" x ¾" x 16¼"

S: 4 stops ¾" x 1¼" x 16¼"

T: 9 spacers for front
¾" x ¾" x 3½"

U: 2 spacers for back
¾" x 1½" x 2¼"

Hardware:

hinges: three 1½" x 3", brass

carriage bolts: eight ¼"-
diameter, 3" long

wood screws: about 100 1½" x
No. 10 stainless flat-head self-
driving for ¾" to 1½" thick
pieces; 100 2½" x No. 12
stainless flat-head self-driving
for 1½" to 1½" pieces

angle irons: two 3" x 3"

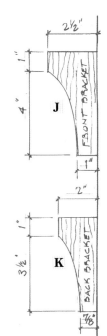

55

bin together on the spot where it will sit. To begin assembling this bin: 1) Build side walls by attaching **C**s to **A**s, leaving a 1"-gap between slats. 2) Attach stops **H** to the appropriate **A**s to create channels for slats. 3) If building the bin in place, dig holes for posts **A** and attach **G**, then all **D**s to the back of them. 4) Roll bin upright, then attach middle back post **A**, and middle front post **A** to **G**. 5) Rock bin onto its back and dig a 3"-deep 7'-long trench for **G** and drop bin into place. 6) Attach spacers **I** to bottoms of 8 **B** slats and 4 **E** slats with carpenter's glue and two galvanized finish nails each, then drop slats into place. 7) Align bin using a level, then tamp down soil around posts. Your bin is ready to be used.

To assemble the compost bench, first put together the base: 1) Attach two stops **S** to the two front end posts **G**, and attach front and back end posts to each other with four side slats **O** per side. Note that front and back **G**s are perpendicular to each other, not parallel. 2) Turn sides upside-down and attach back slats **Q** to back end posts **G**. 3) Attach cross tie **H** to front end posts **G** by screwing through **G**s from the sides, then reinforce with angle irons attached to bottom of **H** and side of **G**. 4) Turn bench upright and dig holes for end posts **G**. Place and level bench and tamp soil around posts. 5) Screw back seat slat **C** to back end posts **G**. 6) Slide front slats **A** and spacers **T** into place. 7) Assemble lid: attach five seat slats **B** ¾" apart to three seat cleats **P** with wood screws from the top; the two side cleats should be about 5½" from the ends of the lid, the third in the center. Place lid on bench. 8) With steel square and pencil, mark level lines down front slats **B** below seat cleats **P** to determine the proper placement of spacers **T** and notches in top slat; then remove slats and spacers and attach spacers to bottoms of three slats **A** using carpenter's glue and finish nails. 9) Notch the top slat **A** with hand-saw and chisel where seat cleats will fall (measure cleat to determine size of notch). Drop slats **A** into place. 10) Attach two hinges to lid and back seat slat **C** in line with seat cleats **P**.

To assemble the arms and back of the bench: 1) Screw front bracket **J** to front arm support **D**, and back bracket **K** to back support **E**. 2) Screw arm rest **I** from the top to front arm support **D** and top of front bracket **J**. 3) Screw arm rest **I** to back support **E** from inside of **E**, then attach arm rest **I** to back bracket **K** through the top of the arm rest. 4) Attach back **M** to left and right back supports **E**. 5) Attach middle back support **F** to back **M**. 6) Center spacers **U** between back supports then attach to the bottom of **M** using carpenter's glue and galvanized nails. 7) Attach back **N** to middle back support **F** and back support **E** just below arms rests **I**. 8) Attach top cap **L** to back supports **E** and middle back support **F** from the top.

Finally, attach arm/back unit to base, screwing front arm supports **D** to end posts **G** with 2½" long wood screws, and back supports **E** to side slats **O** using carriage bolts. Start filling your bench, then sit back and relax. ◎

EVERYTHING YOU NEED (OR DON'T NEED)

TO COMPOST

A Guide to Equipment

BY BETH HANSON

IF YOU ARE A CASUAL, carefree sort, you can just toss your organics into a corner of the garden and they'll slowly become humus without any intervention. But depending on your personality and the amount of time and money you are willing to put into composting, you can also get fully outfitted with an array of composting gadgets and accessories, from auger-shaped aerating tools to herbal compounds designed to inoculate your compost with "medicinal and homeopathic forces."

Below is a description of the composting armamentarium; all of these items are available through a variety of catalog companies (see page 104 for a list of sources) and many can be found in garden centers.

Compost bins The most widely available composting tool is the bin, which can neaten up your yard and speed the composting process by consolidating ingredients. To decide what kind of bin is right for you, determine how much kitchen and yard material you have to compost. Then flip through a few catalogs to get a sense of what various bins look like, how big they are and how much they will set you back. A recent survey of suppliers found bin prices from about $10 (for a paperboard tube) to about $400 (for a heavy-duty metal tumbler).

Make sure the bin you choose is easy to open and allows you easy access for loading and unloading finished compost. Compost bins should be vented to allow air to circulate through the pile, and look for one with a lid if you need to keep

moisture in or out, depending on conditions inside and outside the bin.

Many bins are made from plastic, some from recycled plastic, and come in camouflage colors—green or black. Plastic bins tend to be lighter in weight than those made from other materials. Wood bins usually look great but will very gradually decay as microorganisms that are at work on the compost break down the wood, so look for a naturally rot-resistant wood or replace rotted pieces periodically. Over time, wooden bins may also warp as they are exposed to the elements. You can extend the life of your wooden bin by treating it with a non-toxic weatherproofing substance such as Thompson's WaterSeal.

If rodents or raccoons are a potential problem, make sure that the bin you buy is fully enclosed and "rodent resistant," with openings no larger than ¼-inch

A smattering of the compost bins available commercially: Opposite, clockwise—a standard adjustable bin, the Brave New Composter, the Bio-Stack Composter, a kitchen digester, a slatted bin, the Earth Machine; this page, left, the Tumbler, far right, the ComposTumbler.

to deter mice and ½-inch for rats. Look for bins with rodent screens on the bottom or add your own screen cut from ¼- to ½-inch wire mesh or hardware cloth.

Some bins can be turned; these "tumblers" are designed to make turning the compost easier; some work well and others don't. Be sure the composter you choose is convenient to load and unload and extremely easy to turn because wet compost is heavy. Some recent additions to the tumbler selection include bins shaped like "orbs" that you turn by rolling around the yard and drum-shaped bins that spin on a base covered with little rollers.

Bins may include a number of other features such as slots in the side where you can stick in a pitchfork to loosen the compost, perforated pipes to increase air flow, or doors at the bottom that allow easy access to finished compost.

You can make your own compost bin from lots of different materials—including garbage cans, pallets, and snow-fencing—and in lots of configurations. (You'll find plans for a wooden compost bench and two-

A good fork for turning your compost is probably the first tool you should buy—and could be the last.

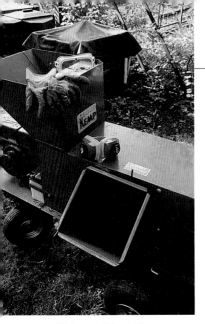

Chipper/shredder

Aerating tool

bin system on page 51, and several of the books on page 102 also include designs for easy-to-make bins.)

Worm bins are a different breed of bin. Most are plastic; some have stacking perforated trays that worms travel up through as they eat, others are basically boxes or trash-can like containers that have spouts to drain excess liquid—compost tea. Some come complete with redworms, others don't. You'll spend from $50 to $150. Again, you can make your own worm bin from lots of different kinds of containers as long as you create holes for air flow.

Shredders and chippers A chipper or shredder is an investment—expect to spend at least $150 for a small shredder and in the thousands of dollars for a heavy-duty commercial machine. But if you're into making hot compost and have lots of big pieces of yard waste—tree limbs, for example—or bags and bags of leaves that you'd like to compost quickly, this may become one of your essential tools.

Machines range from small shredders with half-horsepower motors that run on household current to large, industrial-style chippers with 12-horsepower motors powered by gas, which can reduce 4- to 6-inch thick limbs into tiny chips that will quickly decompose in the compost pile. Combination chipper/shredders are also available.

Shredders are designed to break up leaves, twigs and other light plant material; these are dropped into the shredder's chute and pass by a spinning drum, which has a number of flails (nylon lines) or blades attached to it. Chippers are similar but have one or more blades instead of flails, and can cut larger branches and brush. Shredder/chippers can both shred and chip. Wear protective goggles and earplugs when using this equipment.

Aerating tools An excellent way to get oxygen to the hard-working bacteria in your compost pile is to turn it regularly with a compost fork, a long-handled fork with five or more thin, rounded tines. There are also several other tools that

Use a screen to get rid of large clumps, stones or other debris in your compost.

have been designed especially to aerate compost piles. When thrust into the pile they create long air shafts and stir the contents around a bit; they also minimize your upper-body workout. These compost ventilating tools are basically long metal shafts with handles. Some have small paddles or "wings" that are closed against the shaft as you plunge it into the pile, and which are supposed to open up (they sometimes don't) as you pull it out, mixing the organics. Another type is like a very long corkscrew, which is easy to turn into the pile to make holes. For the lazy composter, there's even a 3-foot-long ventilator that attaches to a power drill. Expect to spend from $15 to $30.

Inoculants The claims made by purveyors of a group of products called bioactivators, inoculants and accelerators are impressive. These additives will "kick start" your compost by "harnessing the power" of various concoctions made from bacteria, fungi, hormones and enzymes and other ingredients such as wheat bran, "granular humates" and seaweed. Inoculants aren't necessarily costly—they average about $6 to $40 per pound (enough for one to two cubic yards of organics). But most of the organics you put in your pile are already covered with the right kinds of organisms. You can also throw handfuls of finished compost or soil, introducing millions of microorganisms and costing you nothing at all.

Screens If you plan to use your compost in potting soil or to topdress the lawn—or for any other purpose where you might not want large clumps, stones or other debris—a screen (also called a sifter, sieve or "riddle") can be very helpful. Small screens have rails that allow them to sit atop a cart or wheelbarrow. One type of larger model is a tub on legs with a screen in the bottom of the tub. You can usually choose the size of the mesh—½-inch or ¼-inch are common

Compost collection pails

A compost thermometer

screens. You can also make your own sieve by stretching a piece of hardware cloth over a wooden frame.

Compost collection pails You can collect kitchen scraps in just about anything, although a container with a lid is probably better than one without. You can also purchase one of several pails designed especially for this purpose. These include a chic galvanized pail with tight-fitting little lid, a brightly colored plastic bucket with a charcoal filter in its lid to eliminate odors and a flower-covered plastic bucket with an optional fruit-fly trap. These range in price from $15 to $35.

Mulching mowers Mulching mowers and mulching kits for regular mowers chop grass into fine pieces; leave this shredded grass on the lawn where it will break down into the soil, or throw it into the compost pile. Regular mowers can be used for mulch mowing too, if you keep the blades very sharp and cut only a third of the grass off at a time. You can also run over leaves or twigs with a mower to turn these into more refined mulches or compost ingredients. Depending on the mower's other features, a "walk-behind" mulching mower can cost from $125 to close to $1,000.

Compost thermometers Stick your pitchfork into the center of your compost pile; if the tines are hot to the touch when you pull the fork out, your pile is cooking. If that doesn't tell you enough about the temperature inside your pile, you probably ought to buy a compost thermometer. If you're hoping to do hot composting to kill weed seeds and pathogens, your pile needs to reach at least 130°F and stay there for a few days. With a thermometer, you can be sure you've gotten it right. These range from 12 inches to 36 inches long and from about $15 to $80.

MYTH-BUSTING

Ten Tall Tales About Composting

BY JOE KEYSER

I T IS A TRIBUTE TO COMPOSTING that humans have taken such a simple, natural process and elevated it through myth and misunderstanding into a form of New-Age alchemy. The spread of these myths has been facilitated by word of mouth, misguided publications from solid waste managers and, worst of all, hard-core marketing. In order to keep composting simple and inexpensive, let's put to rest some of the more popular myths.

1. Compost bins There are scores of weird and wonderful commercial designs available from black plastic cubes with deluxe sliding doors to rotating drums to free-wheeling spheres. The prices range from tens to hundreds of dollars. Advertisements and popular literature lead many composting novices to believe that an enclosed bin is essential. The reality is that heaps or piles work just fine. If you want to keep your pile tidy, consider using wire mesh, or reusing scrap lumber, shipping pallets, cinder

Commercial bins are not essential; in most situations, a compost heap will work just fine.

blocks or snow-fencing. Dry-climate composters might consider using a covered bin to reduce evaporation and moisture loss, while urban composters may decide to contain their compost in sturdy bins with lids, bases and small apertures to keep out pests. (A perforated metal trash can is an excellent choice for city-dwellers.) If you want a prefabricated bin, consider volume before you buy: more money often buys less capacity; the highest capacity models generally sell for less than $40.

Everything you put in the pile is already covered with swarms of bacteria.

2. Bioactivators These bacteria-laden powders and liquids are the snake oil of composting. While they do contain "cultured" strains of bacteria and other additives, the fact is that special inoculants are unnecessary. Recent studies suggest that there are approximately 10 trillion bacteria in a spoonful of garden soil. Every fallen leaf and blade of grass you add to your pile is already covered with hundreds of thousands of bacteria—more than enough to do the job.

Just build a pile and worms will come.

3. Yeast, elixirs and worms There are a number of recommended additives for boosting compost performance, most of which are unsubstantiated or silly. Some practitioners suggest pouring Coca Cola into the pile to increase biological activity; it *will* increase, but mostly in the form of yellow jackets and ants. Adding yeast is also a common practice, but expensive and useless. Adding worms or worm cocoons has grown in popularity due to some confusion with vermicomposting. Worms do a tremendous amount of good, but need not be purchased or transplanted by the average backyard composter: just build a pile and they will come. (But see "From Pits to Piles," page 40, for some situations in which it makes sense to add worms.)

4. Fertilizer Adding fertilizer to increase the nitrogen content of a pile is wasteful and expensive. More importantly, synthetically derived fertilizers contain high salt levels and other compounds (perhaps even pesticides), which are harmful to worms and microorganisms; they may impair the nitrogen-fixing ability of the bacteria and short-circuit the nitrogen cycle. If you feel that you must add nitrogen, perhaps to a pile made up of only carbon-rich leaves, always try to use organic sources first: spent grounds from a coffee shop, a neighbor's grass clippings, agricultural manures or dried blood.

If you build the pile with lasagna-style layers, you may have anaerobic decay.

5. Lime Many gardeners with a high proportion of acid-rich materials to compost mistakenly add lime to their pile to produce compost with a balanced pH. Unfortunately, adding ground limestone will turn your compost ecosystem into an ammonia factory, with nitrogen rapidly lost as a noxious gas. Finished compost is almost always nearly neutral.

6. Odors A properly built and managed compost pile should smell like the humus-sweet duff of a forest floor. Odors result primarily from mistakes: trying to compost grass clippings by themselves, adding too many food scraps (or the wrong types of food) and allowing too much water to get into the pile or too little air, both of which will lead to anaerobic conditions.

7. Rodents and pests Compost piles almost never attract pests if they contain only yard trimmings. Properly constructed compost piles fall well behind bird feeders, outdoor pet-food bowls, pet feces and trash containers as rodent attracters. Adding food to your pile will make it somewhat more attractive to pests, but only if you manage scraps improperly—by dumping them on the top of a pile or bin, for example. But because pests are more problematic in urban areas, composters there might want to avoid adding food altogether or use a worm box or a completely enclosed bin. In fact, some composters in dense urban areas find that an enclosed compost bin is necessary even when they're composting just yard trimmings.

8. Layers Building a compost pile by layering browns/greens/browns/greens—then leaving your bin in a nice, orderly lasagna style—will lead to layers of anaerobic activity where the greens (nitrogen-rich, wet) are clumped together and little activity at all where the browns (carbon-rich, dry) are clumped together. If you're building a pile all at once, throw in an armful of browns, then an armful of greens, and add a little water as you go if your materials are dry. Then mix, stir, and fluff after every few additions for a hard-working compost stew.

9. Fourteen-day compost A number of magazine ads have hoodwinked well-intentioned gardeners into thinking that they must produce compost in 14 days.

Wait a month after your pile *looks* like compost before using it.

Such expectations are unrealistic and unworthy. Decomposition takes time. While producing compost quickly has some merit, no one should feel compelled to purchase chipper-shredders or other elaborate equipment. In fact, even if material *looks* like compost after several weeks, it still requires an additional one-month maturation period before it should be used in the garden.

10. Compost calculus For years, books, periodicals and composting brochures have obsessed on carbon-to-nitrogen ratios. Regrettably, the arcane charts, tables and formulas provided overwhelm many gardeners. In truth, compost piles thrive when different types of material (moist and dry, green and brown) are mixed together. And while ratios are fine for compost hobbyists, regular gardeners need only remember that all organic materials will compost in a timely manner given some prudent attention.

COMPOSTING COAST TO COAST

Tips for Difficult Climes

BY BETH HANSON

COMPOST HAPPENS, as the saying goes. But what you happen to have to put in the pile depends on where you live—as does the amount of rainfall you get, the range of the ambient temperature and the needs of your soil. Climate also has a big effect on the rate of growth of microorganisms, which in turn affect the rate of decomposition and the longevity of humus in the soil. Here, composting experts from four major climatic regions of the continent, which include some of the trickier climes for composting—the South, North/Central states, Southwest and Northwest—pass on some of the tips they give to composters in their areas.

COMPOSTING IN THE SOUTH

The big challenge for southern composters is hot weather, according to Trecia Neal, a biologist and

Whatever initial ingredients you start with, local conditions will dictate the terms of decomposition.

Gardens in the coastal plains of the South are rich in pine needles, which break down slowly in the compost pile but make an excellent mulch.

composting expert at the Fernbank Science Center in Atlanta. The heat in the South dries compost piles out very quickly. So while she recommends that composters use a bin made of wooden pallets or of cement blocks because both allow easy access to the pile, she suggests covering three sides of the bin with plywood so that less moisture can escape. In hot weather, Southern composters should remember to water their piles often, says Neal.

Gardens in the coastal plains of the South are rich in pine needles, which Neal advises using as a mulch, while gardens inland have lots of deciduous trees and a long leaf season—"Atlantans rake from September through May," says Neal. She advises gardeners to reduce leaf volume to manageable levels by shredding or mowing their leaves. One clever way to do this is to start mowing at the edge of the yard and work in a circle toward the center, shredding leaves in the process. Instead of 12 bags of leaves scattered all over the yard, you'll have four bags of shredded leaves in the center, which can be composted or used as a mulch.

Compost breaks down quickly in the South—both in the pile and after application—because of the heat and humidity. "In Atlanta, we have red clay soil, which supports only weeds unless it is amended seriously with compost," says Neal. "For new plots, I recommend double-digging and replacing half of the volume of soil with compost, but keep some of the clay because it helps the soil hold water," she advises. Once planting beds are established, they need an annual topdressing of a couple of inches of compost.

Southern composters who don't maintain their piles rigorously may encounter fire ants, says Neal; if they're in the pile, turning it will be a nasty, painful experience. But if your pile has been invaded, pull on some gloves and turn it anyway.

Composters in frigid northern climes can retrofit most types of bins with styrofoam to keep heat from escaping.

COMPOSTING IN THE NORTH & CENTRAL STATES

In the northern regions of the continent the growing season is relatively short, and the compost pile is more likely to freeze solid during the long, cold winters, says Robin Tench, compost advisor at the Metroworks Department in Toronto, Ontario. "In the spring, people call in a panic when they find the kitchen scraps they've thrown onto their pile all winter thawing out, surrounded by flies, and starting to smell pretty sour."

To keep the pile from freezing through the North's freeze and thaw cycles, Tench advises composters to get a hot compost going in early fall and to keep it cooking during the winter by adding shredded leaves each time they add food scraps. Tench keeps her own pile steaming all winter long. "Keep a constant supply of leaves on hand by shredding them with a lawn mower or weed whacker in the fall; bag them and keep them by the pile," she says. Even if your pile doesn't get steaming hot, add browns with the food scraps and they'll decompose slowly together through the winter. She also advises composters to add red wrigglers to the pile, because they'll help break it down more quickly.

For those who have tried and not succeeded at hot composting, Tench suggests keeping the pile warm by insulating all sides of the bin with 2-inch-thick pieces of styrofoam. "Almost any bin, but the wooden ones most easily, can be retrofitted with styrofoam," Tench says.

Because the growing season around Toronto is relatively short, the soil life is not particularly active, so compost breaks down gradually. "We recommend that people work a half-inch of compost into the soil in the spring and top- and sidedress through the season with a half inch more."

COMPOSTING IN THE SOUTHWEST

People who live in Santa Fe and its surrounds have 200-plus days of sun each year, says Marcia Barton, gardening expert at Seeds of Change, as well as very low humidity and little rain. One of the big challenges for composters in this climate is that they have little to compost—raw ingredients are hard to come by, she says. "We're in a high semi-desert climate here, and people don't have lawns so there's no grass; there are no deciduous trees so we don't have leaves and brushy stuff, and most people don't create enough kitchen scraps for a whole pile."

Barton imports the ingredients for her own pile from nearby farms, using horse manure instead of what she considers more ideal—cow manure—because there are no dairy cows around. She mixes the horse manure with straw, watering the pile with each addition.

To protect the pile from the arid air and heat, she advises composters to build their pile in the shade and then to cover it with a thick layer of straw or plastic. Using a bin would keep the pile from losing moisture, "but I just make mine with bales of straw turned on their sides as the walls," she says, which act as insulation.

Because organic matter oxidizes so quickly in the intense sunlight and aridity of the Southwest, "we need to use a lot more compost to amend the soil—two to four times as much compost as in more temperate parts of the country," she says. "I recommend that people use a lot of compost at the beginning of the season and then not top- or sidedress during the rest of the year."

Make sure that the compost you use does not contain high levels of salt, as these will build up in the soil and harm your plants. Be especially careful when buying commercial compost, as it is more likely to contain high levels of salts (salt levels should not exceed 5 mmhos/cm).

Composters in the Southwest have to cope with much more sun and much less humidity and rain than composters in other parts of the country.

COMPOSTING IN THE NORTHWEST

Along the maritime coast of the Northwest, winters are generally wet rather than freezing, while, contrary to common images of the region as damp and misty, summers are sometimes dry—enough so that composters must water their piles, according to Michael Levenston, executive director of City Farmer in Vancouver, British Columbia.

In the coastal regions of the Northwest, most people have an abundance of greens but probably not browns year-round. To assure a steady supply of browns, "we tell people to bag their leaves in the fall and to keep them near the compost pile, covered up, and to add them to the pile throughout the year as they add greens." The city has an abundance of trees and collects compostables such as leaves, so throughout the fall there are bags of them out on the curb for the taking; those who need extras can grab a couple of bags from their neighbors. During the winter cover food scraps with the leaves, and use them in other seasons to cover greens.

Gardeners along the coast of the Northwest have an abundance of "green" compostables.

Levenston recommends that composters use fully enclosed bins—otherwise the piles will get soaked through from rain. "Cover all six sides of the pile—top, bottom and sides—and make sure that your bin does not have any holes larger than ½ inch if rats are a potential problem and ¼ inch if mice are around." City Farmer recommends inexpensive plastic, wood and wire mesh bins, and emphasizes aerating with a compost poker.

"We tell people to incorporate compost in the soil when they are about to plant a bed, which may be several times during the growing season because of our weather. They should add compost each time, working an inch or two into the surface of the soil. We also recommend topdressing or mulching throughout the season, using one to two inches around the plants and letting the rain work it in."

LET WORMS DO YOUR WORK

Composting Indoors

BY MARY APPELHOF

WORMS IN THE KITCHEN! Whatever for? Because people in every climate and in any size dwelling can compost food scraps year-round by turning worms loose on their scraps. This process is called *vermicomposting*. Small indoor worm composting systems can handle up to five pounds of food scraps each week, producing 10 to 15 gallons of vermicompost per year—nutrient-rich humus for garden and houseplants.

Vermicomposting offers several advantages: you can compost in very small spaces—as small as 2 cubic feet—both indoors and out; the worms do all the heavy work, turning and aerating the pile; and the end product of worm composting, vermicompost, has higher nutrient value for plants than regular compost.

Worm bins produce 10-15 gallons of compost yearly.

Redworms chow down on the organics you bury in moistened bedding in the bin and transform it to black, odorless worm manure called worm castings.

To get your worm composting system going, all you need is a suitable container, bedding, redworms and a proper environment. The worms, along with millions of microorganisms, chow down on the organics you bury in moistened bedding in the bin and transform it to black, odorless worm manure called worm castings. As long as the system has enough oxygen and moisture, and temperatures remain between freezing and 90°F, the bedding disappears, the food scraps vanish and the worms multiply. Periodically, harvest the vermicompost—a mixture of worm castings, partially decomposed organics and uneaten bedding—and use it as top dressing for houseplants, as an ingredient in potting mixes or as an immediate source of fertilizer for transplants and seed beds.

HOUSING YOUR WORMS

All sorts of containers will work as worm bins—but aeration is a must. Wooden bins with half-inch holes in the sides or bottom work well, but these tend to be heavy. Plastic storage containers are another good option, but you will have to drill holes in the sides and lids. (Some people cover these holes with screening to keep worms and bedding in, but this isn't necessary.) Plastic containers are usually less expensive than wood, but tend to keep in a good deal of moisture. If the bin's contents seems too wet, add more dry bedding. You can purchase commercial vermicomposting units that have been designed to address all of these problems—but these will cost more than the ones you adapt with your drill.

Add shredded newspaper to the bin—about 5 pounds for a 12-gallon bin.

Worms need grit for their gizzards, so add about a quart of soil to the bin.

MAKING THE BED

Worm bedding holds moisture, provides worms with a place to live and work and gives you a place to bury garbage. Surprisingly, soil is not a big component of worm bedding. Worms *do* need soil, but only in small portions—about a quart per bin—which provides grit for their gizzards. A loamy soil is ideal for this purpose, but most garden soils will do just fine. The soil you add also contains bacteria, fungi and other microorganisms that will inoculate the medium with a diverse group of organisms—more diverse than food scraps and bedding alone provide. Shredded newspaper, machine-shredded office paper, leaf mold, horse manure or mixtures of these materials make satisfactory, free beddings. Add water to the bedding so that it is damp, but not wringing wet. If paper crinkles, it is too dry. For a 12-gallon (16" x 19" x 12") bin you will need about 5 pounds of newspaper. Shred the sheets by tearing parallel to the center fold until you have strips about 1 to 2 inches wide and the length of the paper.

Coconut fiber (coir, coco-peat) is now on the market as a worm bedding (and also as a growing mix). Coir comes in compressed blocks, which you place in the amount of water specified on the instructions; the fiber will quickly expand as it absorbs the water and becomes a nice worm bedding. Coir, a waste-product of the coconut industry, is a disposal problem throughout the tropics. Although the environmental costs associated with its transportation are a concern, use of this renewable resource makes more sense than using peat moss. Some vermicomposters recommend peat, but it can be too acid and is a non-renewable resource—most is extracted from Canadian bogs at a rate faster than nature can replace it.

WHICH WORMS?

To succeed with worm composting you need to make sure you have the right worms for the job—those whose natural niche is to quickly process large amounts of organics. Redworms are best suited for this work. They are known variously as manure worms, red wrigglers and tiger worms, among other common names. To reduce the confusion caused by local worm names, use the scientific name for the species, *Eisenia fetida* (these redworms are striped) and its close relative, *Eisenia andrei* (these are not striped). Most redworm cultures available from commercial growers are one or the other, or a mixture of these species. These worms process about half their body weight in food in a day, reproduce quickly at temperatures of 65°-75°F, and can consume a wide range of foods. *Eisenia* species do not make

After adding soil and kitchen scraps to the pile, cover with more paper.

If the paper is still a little dry, sprinkle more water on top.

extensive burrow systems, so they don't mind being turned and dug up and moved around in the bin as you bury garbage. If you live in a cold climate, keep your bin inside during winter so that the worms don't freeze.

Don't populate your bin with worms from your garden. If you *have* used them, you probably decided that vermicomposting doesn't work—but you just chose the wrong worm. Soil-dwelling worms have different jobs to do—aerating the soil as they make burrows, mixing organics with soil and along the way creating a spongy texture in soil, which makes it hold water better than compacted soil. And these worms won't process as much organic material as you would put in a worm bin, and won't reproduce quickly, if at all.

WHAT TO FEED THEM?

You can put all kinds of organics in your worm bin, but most people succeed best with vegetable and fruit scraps—lettuce, cabbage, potato peels, leftovers (avoid highly acidic foods; for example, those containing lots of vinegar), tea leaves, coffee grounds (bags and filters are okay, too). Egg shells add calcium and other nutrients; they will break down faster when pulverized with a rolling pin. You can also add citrus rinds, but only in small amounts. Large doses of citrus cause odors and can kill the worm population. The high protein content in meat, bones and dairy products is likely to cause odor problems, and can attract flies, rats or other pests, so don't add these to your worm bin.

You might expect to smell some pretty offensive odors when you begin burying food scraps in a small worm bin, but you will be surprised at how little odor there is. If you *do* notice some bad smells, disturb the bedding as little as possible when you bury organics, cover the waste with bedding and deposit it in different spots each time. Odors can also result if your bedding is too moist. If the bin seems to be soggy and waterlogged, add dry shredded bedding and let the moisture redistribute itself. You may also get odors if you don't have a big enough worm population.

Fruit flies may also be attracted to your bin. If you find them swarming around the box, bury all food items well when you add them to the box, or wrap them in newspaper so that the flies can't get to them. If you decide to wrap, you will probably have to add a little more water.

ASSEMBLING THE BIN

Once you've got all of your ingredients—an aerated container, a quart of soil, a pound or so of redworms, bedding and food scraps—you can easily set up the bin. Put the shredded paper in the bin, add the soil, then add about 1½-2 gallons of water, mixing until most of the paper is wet. Empty the worms and the medium they were shipped in on top of the bedding; they will quickly move down into the paper away from the light. Draw enough bedding aside to make room for a quart-sized container of garbage and chuck it into the hole. Spread bedding over the garbage and put the lid on the container. That's all there is to it! From here on in bury garbage once or twice a week, in a different spot each time. Monitor the bedding for adequate moisture. If it's dry, add water.

After eight weeks or so, you will have nutrient-rich worm castings.

After several weeks you will notice that the food scraps disappear, some kinds faster than others. The worms will reproduce. The first sign will be small, yellowish cocoons, somewhat smaller than a mung bean. After two or three months, you may have twice as many worms as you started with. You can use them to go fishing, or help a neighbor set up a bin or just leave them in your bin. Overpopulation will not be a problem.

WORM CASTINGS

When the material in the bin becomes dark and crumbly, remove some of the vermicompost. You can take out about two-thirds of the vermicompost to use as topdressing on your houseplants or as an ingredient in potting mixes. Or my favorite method is to deposit a handful of vermicompost—worms and all—in the hole I make for transplants such as broccoli and tomatoes. The vermicompost nutrients will be right in the root zone of the developing plant. The redworms may not live long in this foreign soil environment, but while they do, they will make more castings and secrete nitrogen-rich slime. When they die, their bodies will add another shot of nitrogen to the soil.

Plants fertilized with worm castings thrive, providing beauty, pleasure and good food. And the residues from these plants can be put back in the worm bin to be recycled again in a convenient, natural, and environmentally sound way.

MICRO-COMPOST

Making Humus in Small Spaces

BY PATRICIA JASAITIS

WHY WOULD A GARDENER working in tight quarters, whose priority is *growing* things, ever give up precious real estate for *rotting* things? Then again, how could a gardener pass up the chance to create more soil when there's never enough? This fundamental conflict is one that many space-deprived gardeners struggle with.

Suppose you garden on a patio, balcony, rooftop or in a small backyard. Consider the amount of work you do hauling garden clippings to the trash, and then buying and hauling bagged, commercially composted organic matter and fertilizer back into the garden. Finally, consider how little space and effort you would need to collect and make use of your garden waste and food scraps. You may decide that a little compost pile makes sense after all.

Here are some suggestions for ways to squeeze organic recycling into unlikely spaces.

MULCHING

In any type of garden, if you do just a bit of work with the pruning shears, you can make a nice mulch out of twigs, small branches and hedge trimmings—simply cut them into 1- to 3-inch long pieces. You can also lay whole twigs, branches, Christmas tree boughs and even weeds right on the soil where you won't mind a coarse blanket.

DIGGING IN

Some gardeners recycle their garden and food leftovers without a compost bin, by simply incorporating materials directly into the soil. Open a hole 6 to 8 inches deep, toss in the organic materials and top with soil. Trees and shrubs grown in planters respond well to this bonsai-like scheme, which is mildly disturbing to the roots but replenishes organic matter. Greedy fruit trees especially appreciate these "treats."

POTS AND PLANTERS

If you keep plants in pots around your garden, why not do your composting in a pot, too? With containers available in so many shapes, styles, sizes and materials, something is

City soils are often poor and benefit greatly when compost is added.

bound to fit in with your garden. If you have a small patio or balcony, a pot 12 inches tall and wide may suffice, while gardeners with larger rooftops and urban backyards may need one or more 18-inch planters or whiskey barrels.

Make sure the bottom has drainage holes and find a cover, such as an inverted, oversized pot saucer, to prevent materials from drying out or getting too soggy from rain. Start by laying a thick layer of absorbent materials as a base, such as old soil, finished compost, leaves or shredded newspaper. Add garden trimmings and weeds, sprinkle them with water and bury food scraps below the surface. Miniature compost piles will decompose slowly and without a build-up of heat.

Expand to two pots and you can keep two different stages of compost going—one pot with compost that's nearly ready to use, another accumulating the new additions. "Turning" compost in a pot is fun; it feels a lot like tossing a salad or stirring a stew.

Trash cans are great bins for small spaces.

WINDOW BOXES

For apartment-dwellers with no balcony, garden or rooftop, a window box can be the receptacle for spent plants and trimmings, and with some chopping, a small amount of food scraps as well. Simply tuck organics between growing plants, or keep an unplanted window box partially filled with potting soil to collect more materials. You may not be able to compost all of your food scraps using this system, but at least some will go toward improving the soil. My own compost bin for the moment—a plastic tool box—sits on my windowsill filled with newspaper strips, food scraps and old soil.

If you plan to compost on your windowsill, please think about the safety of those below! Bolt down or wire the window box so it cannot fall and shower a passerby with its contents.

COMPOST TOWERS

A narrow tower of chicken wire or wire mesh, ready to capture weeds and trimmings, can be nestled among plants in a garden where it will be hardly noticeable. The smallest columns I've seen range from 1 to 2 feet tall and 8 to 12 inches in diameter. Because each unit is light and narrow, you can scatter a few of these mini-bins throughout the garden and move them as needed. A tall, skinny tower, dug into the soil a bit to stabilize it, could form a trellis for annual flowering vines to climb up the sides.

You can also stack milk crates three to five tall, and fill them with compost materials. Put the oldest, most rotted material in the lowest crate, a younger stage of decay in the middle layer and the newest organics in the top crate. To harvest finished compost, take the bottom crate out, empty it and then replace it at the top.

Laundry hampers have built-in vents.

GARBAGE CANS AND LAUNDRY HAMPERS

Plastic and metal garbage cans make great compost bins for small spaces, on open ground or pavement. Lots of sizes and styles are available in plastic or metal, stationary or on wheels, with or without lids. Drill or hammer ¼- to ½-inch holes all around the outside and the bottom of the can. One garbage-can company even makes a metal "incinerator" can with pre-drilled holes. Or try a laundry hamper, which has built-in aeration vents and sometimes a handy flip-lid. A tray or saucer placed below the bin will catch run-off, which you can pour into the garden like compost tea. If you compost in a wheeled trash can, you can store it in a hidden spot and roll it to the garden as necessary.

COMMERCIAL BINS AND TUMBLERS

Rooftop gardens and backyards may produce enough garden debris for a "regular"-size compost bin, which you can build yourself or purchase. One commercially available bin is very narrow—with 23-inch sides. The look of the commercial black plastic bins works surprisingly well in most gardens. If rodents are a concern, look for a bin with an optional rodent screen to enclose the bottom; the screen also helps keep materials contained if the bin is placed on pavement instead of open soil. If you have a large amount of materials to compost, you may be able to justify the cost of a possibly high-priced tumbler.

WORM BINS

Worm bins, indoors or out, are obvious solutions for small-space composting (see "Let Worms Do Your Work," page 73, for information on composting

This bench holds 4½ cubic feet.

indoors). If you plan to compost outdoors and live in a cold climate, your worm bin should be on the large side, so that the amount of bedding is sufficient to insulate the redworms over winter. You could also try using a smaller bin if you can provide the worms with access to the soil, so that they can retreat below ground temporarily during inclement weather.

You can perch on this bench and compost, too. We've included plans for an even more relaxing compost bench—with a back and arms—on page 51, as well as plans for a two-bin system.

SOCIAL COMPOST

Another way to compost without any outdoor space of your own is to share a compost bin with the other residents of your apartment building or townhouse complex. You can set up bins along the side of a building, on pavement or on a roof, and use the finished compost in street plantings or donate them to other gardens.

COMPOST BENCH

If you still can't stand the idea of composting, why don't you sit on it? Make a compost bench for your small garden! A bench gives you a chance to pursue two activities—rotting and resting—in one spot. On page 51, you'll find complete plans for a comfortable, attractive and very useful compost bench and a list of the materials you'll need. (You'll also find plans for a two-bin system.) With a compost structure so gorgeous, you may not mind sharing the space.

MAKE THE MOST OF YOUR COMPOST

Using Compost in the Garden

BY MIRANDA SMITH

YOU'LL EXPERIENCE REAL PLEASURE when you begin to use your compost in your garden. It won't take you long to discover that good compost benefits your soil and plants in ways that no other amendment or fertilizer can. Well-made compost can be used in myriad ways—as a soil conditioner, a nutrient source, a disease suppressive, a mulch or the primary ingredient in potting soils. But not all composts are created equal.

Three factors determine the qualities of particular composts: the initial ingredients, the type of composting process used and the length of time and conditions under which the compost cured. To a large extent, you can customize your composts by simply changing one or another of these elements. To make the most of any type of compost, you'll have to match it with the benefits you want from it. Some composts, for example, are best used as fertilizers for your plants

Compost can be used myriad ways: as a soil conditioner, a nutrient source, a disease suppressive and a mulch.

while almost all composts improve the water-holding capacity of the soil but may not enhance the nutrient content significantly.

COMPOST AS A SOIL CONDITIONER

All composts help to condition soil by improving its structure. A good soil has what is called a "crumb" structure; particles within the soil are bound together in relatively stable little crumbs, or aggregates. The irregular shapes of the aggregates make lots of space for air and water. Some of the components in compost encourage soil aggregates to bind together, and the more tightly bound a soil's aggregates are, the better it can withstand the onslaught of a rainstorm or footfall.

Whether you have loamy, sandy or clay soil, amend with compost.

Because compost promotes the formation of aggregates, which create spaces between crumbs, it helps to loosen compacted clay soils and makes sandy ones more water-retentive. The surface of a well-composted soil doesn't form a crust, no matter what the weather, so raindrops and irrigation water can penetrate it more easily, giving a soil some insurance against erosion. And because composted soil holds water well, it can protect plants during drought conditions.

Lighter, more crumbly soils are much easier to work than compacted ones. If you use a tiller to incorporate cover crops and prepare the garden every year, your tiller will be doing all the work and you may not notice the difference at first. But after only a few years of compost application, all tilling and digging operations will be much easier than they once were. You may even find that you can forego the yearly tilling in favor of a fast session with a spading fork.

Over the years, composted soils also become gradually darker. Even soils that were once light-colored and sandy begin to develop a dark brown hue. This color change affects your garden in surprising ways. Dark-colored soils absorb

Apply a half to a full inch of compost over all the growing beds each year.

more light energy than light-colored ones, and store more heat. They help soil to heat much more quickly in the spring, decrease the day to night temperature fluctuations enough so that plants grow more quickly and keep the soil warmer in the fall, extending the growing season somewhat.

You can derive all of these soil-conditioning benefits by adding all types of compost, no matter what the ingredients, composting process and length of the curing stage. Just apply a half to a full inch of compost over all the growing beds each year. You can use the compost as a mulch or till it into the top several inches of soil. (See "Composting Coast to Coast," page 67, for tips on amending with compost in difficult climes.)

COMPOST AS A SLOW-RELEASE FERTILIZER

At first, you may be tempted to think of the nutritional components of compost in the same way you think of those in chemical fertilizers—as percentages of nitrogen, phosphorus and potassium (N-P-K) plus other elements. But while this way of rating a compost is useful, it doesn't tell the whole story. Compost may have low N-P-K ratings, but is nonetheless the best fertilizer available, for many reasons.

Not all the materials in a compost are fully broken down by the time it is considered "finished." When you spread it on soil, you are adding a diverse and numerous population of decomposing microorganisms as well as food supplies for them. As they gradually continue the decay process, they slowly release nutrients into the soil.

A compost made primarily of manure or kitchen waste will release about half of its nutrients during the first season after application. In the second and subsequent seasons, smaller proportions are released because the remaining material is more resistant to decay. This compost may be releasing fewer nutrients, but it is still conditioning the soil and stimulating plant growth.

HOW COMPOST INGREDIENTS AFFECT NUTRIENT CONTENT

Beginning composters often assume that a yearly compost application will supply all of their plants' nutritional needs. But composts vary in the types and amounts of nutrients they contain. A compost made of leaves and yard trimmings is likely to be high in trace elements, for example, and low in available N, P and K. Generally, the best composts for use as fertilizers have a high proportion of manure and/or kitchen scraps. And the more diverse the original ingredients, the more complete the resulting nutrient supply.

Only fully finished composts are good fertilizers. A compost made with a large fraction of well-shredded carbonaceous materials such as autumn leaves or sawdust bedding can seem finished before it is. Because the carbon content is so high, these composts frequently run out of nitrogen before all the carbonaceous materials have been broken down. Consequently, they seem finished because they don't reheat after being turned. If you apply a high-carbon compost to your garden, the decomposing microorganisms will scavenge nitrogen from the soil to sustain themselves while they finish the composting. In this way, they borrow nutrients from, rather than contribute them to, your plants. Over time, the balance of nutrients returns and nitrogen will become available to the plants. A cress test, as described opposite, will help you determine the nutrient level of your compost.

USE COMPOST THROUGHOUT THE SEASON

Soils that have been robbed of organic matter by a reliance on chemical fertilizers rarely contain either the microorganisms necessary to make good use of compost, or the reserve fertility that will see crops through a season. As you apply compost over a few years, this situation will change, of course. But without addi-

IS YOUR COMPOST FINISHED YET?: THE CRESS AND BAG TESTS

A "cress test" is the fastest way to determine if a compost is ready to be used. Cress is very susceptible to phytotoxins, germinates within only four or five days and has a very high germination rate.

Conduct the test by counting out two batches of 25 cress seeds each. Fill two flats with media, one with straight compost, and the other with a conventional potting mixture. Plant the flats, water, cover and sit back and wait for germination.

Keep track of the speed and numbers of plants that germinate in each flat. If fewer than 80 percent (20 seeds) sprout in the compost-filled flat, your compost is probably not yet ready to be used. But if you get a good germination rate, you can be certain it is. You might also want to track the progress of your seedlings to check on nutrient release. Feed the seeds in the potting soil with a natural fertilizer made from fish emulsion and seaweed and give the compost seedlings only water. Within a few weeks, your baby cress plants will show you why all gardeners grow to love compost.

You can also test the readiness of your soil using a "bag test." Put a handful of compost in a zip-lock bag and leave it in there for a week or so. Then open the bag and sniff. If you smell ammonia or sourness, the microorganisms in your compost are still at work and you need to let it mature; test it again in several weeks.

tional inputs, plants could be nutrient-deficient during the soil-building period.

Begin your compost-adding program by spreading at least an inch over all growing areas before you plant in the spring, and turn the compost into the top several inches of the soil. This early in the year the soil will be so cool that only the already-soluble nutrients are available; compensate for this by soaking the rootballs of your earliest transplants in a dilution of liquid fish emulsion. Within only a few weeks time, though, the soil will begin to heat. As the soil warms to temperatures of 50°F and above, the microorganisms will begin to transform the other nutrients in the compost into available forms—but since only 50 percent of the nutrients in the compost will be made available over the season, it's entirely possible that supplies won't be adequate. Supplement your original compost application by sidedressing the heavy-feeding crops such as squash, corn, tomatoes and even broccoli with either a half-inch layer of compost or a blended organic fertilizer each month during the growing season.

AMENDING POOR SOILS

Soils vary so much that it is impossible to give a blanket recipe for compost applications over the years. However, it's safe to make some ballpark suggestions. For the first five to seven years, nutrient-depleted, compacted and/or very sandy soils generally require at least an inch of compost over all growing areas every spring. In addition, they will require either a blended organic fertilizer or additional compost applications once or twice during the season, and cover crops over the winter months. After this time, the soil may have improved so much that a maintenance application of a half-inch in the spring is adequate and only

the heavy-feeding crops will need supplementation during the season. You will see a visible difference in the soil—it will look darker and looser-textured. Compost-amended soil will also have higher levels of nutrients when tested at a lab, and a good test will show increased organic matter content.

Spray plants susceptible to disease—tomatoes, lilacs, and roses, for example—with compost tea every two weeks during the beginning and middle of the season.

Side-dress heavy-feeding crops such as squash, corn, tomatoes and broccoli with a half-inch layer of compost monthly during the growing season.

Soils that are not depleted or too sandy or compacted also require inch-deep applications for the first years and some supplemental fertilization during the summer. The difference is one of time. While a poor soil may take seven years to begin regaining health and better tilth, a decent soil can be improved in only three or four. Let common sense, and a few soil tests, be your guide in deciding when to put soil on a maintenance rather than a soil-building regime.

COMPOST AS A FALL FERTILIZER

Compost used for spring fertilizing must be fully finished and cured to do a good job. But in the fall, you can spread material that is not yet cured. If you have no place to store compost over the winter and must make use of it, try the following: on areas where frost-tender crops have just died, pull their residues and then apply a half-inch or less of your uncured compost. Work it into the soil and plant a cover crop. You can also spread uncured compost over a vigorously growing cover crop and let the rain and snow work it into the soil over the winter. By spring the compost will be contributing both nutrients and soil-building qualities to your garden.

COMPOST AS A MULCH

The ideal mulch returns organic matter to the soil while moderating soil temperatures, retaining moisture and suppressing weeds. All finished composts can do all this, but composts made primarily from leaves and yard wastes are the best choice for mulches because of their lighter finished texture.

When you are making a compost for a mulch, avoid, if at all possible, using initial ingredients that carry weed seeds. One way to ensure that you are

When mulching with compost, avoid composts that may contain weed seeds.

not adding scores of viable seeds to your garden beds is to get the temperature in your compost pile to remain at 150°F for at least three days. Maintaining compost temperatures this high can be difficult. Turn the compost frequently—enough so that you move all of the outside material to the hot interior. Other tips for hot composting are included in "From Pits to Piles," page 40. When the compost is finished, cover it while it is curing so that no new weed seeds can blow onto it.

Some mulches are added to the soil in fairly deep layers, but because the particle size in compost is so small, you need only add an inch or two at the beginning of the season after the soil has warmed in the spring. You may need to add another couple of inches before the fall, because by then microorganisms will have decomposed a great deal of the original material. Take care not to pile the mulch against trunks of trees and shrubs or the bark may rot. If the mulch is too deep, it will prevent air from getting into the soil and may smother tree roots.

Weeds like compost mulches. Even if the material contained no viable weed seeds when you put it down, some seeds are sure to blow in. Fortunately, a compost mulch is so light-textured that you can easily pull any weeds that sprout. But you do have to stay on top of them. If you let weed roots grow down below the compost layer, they won't be so easy to pull.

PREVENTING DISEASE

Gardeners have suspected for many, many years that composts suppress several fungal plant diseases, but only in the last decade have researchers con-

HOW MUCH COMPOST TO USE IN THE GARDEN?

WHERE:	HOW MUCH TO APPLY:
New lawns	1"-2" mixed into top 4"-6" of soil
Reseeded lawns	1" mixed into top 2"-3" of soil
Top-dressing for existing lawns	⅛"-¼" spread uniformly
Top-dressing for vegetables, flowers, shrubs	1"-2" spread uniformly
Groundcover and annual planting beds	3" mixed into top 6" of soil
Garden soil	1"-3" mixed into top 6"-8" of soil
Around shrubs	3" mixed into top 6" of soil
Potting-soil mix	25-30% by volume
Mulch for deciduous trees, rose beds	3"-4" spread uniformly
Mulch for vegetables, annual and perennial planting beds	2"-3" spread uniformly
Mulch for exposed slopes	2"-4" of coarse compost (¾"-1½" grade) spread uniformly

*Note: The application rates in this table represent ranges reported in the published litera-
ture on compost. Approximately 1,000 pounds of compost is equivalent to one cubic
yard of compost. One inch of compost spread over one acre is equivalent to approximately 65 tons of compost. Where appropriate, these rates represent annual applications. See "How Much Compost do I Need?," page 100, to determine how much compost to acquire.*

Source: Richard Kashmanian and Joe Keyser

93

firmed this. To take advantage of this quality, make a fully finished compost as usual. Then soak a quart of it in a covered 5-gallon bucket for five to 15 days. Strain the resulting liquid, dilute until it is the color of tea and spray it over plant leaves very early in the morning. Use this tea as part of an overall disease suppression regime that is appropriate for your plants. Compost tea is also a good source of the major plant nutrients—especially tea made from manures.

This tea only *prevents* diseases, it will not *cure* them. Spray extremely susceptible plants such as tomatoes, lilacs or roses every two weeks or so during the beginning and middle of the season. But be careful—compost tea contains a high proportion of easily

Compost is excellent in potting soil.

assimilated nutrients. If plants begin to show signs of nutrient excess such as weak, sappy growth, leaves that are too large and lush or unusual attractiveness to aphids, cut back on the sprays.

COMPOST IN POTTING SOILS

Compost makes potting soils that hold water and nutrients, drain well and promote excellent growth. A recipe that includes a third compost, a third expanded coconut fiber (coir, coco peat) and a sixth vermiculite and a sixth perlite usually produces a medium that will supply balanced nutrients for at least six weeks.

But compost quality is imperative when it's used in potting soils. You must use fully finished and well-cured composts. If your compost is lumpy or coarse, screen it before adding to the soil mix. As many people have discovered to their dismay, some of the by-products formed during the composting process are phytotoxic, or poisonous to plants. These compounds are gone by the time a compost is finished and cured, so it's wise to test a compost before using it in a potting soil (see "Is Your Compost Finished Yet?" on page 89).

COMMERCIAL COMPOSTS

A Buyer's Guide

BY ROD TYLER

I F YOU NEED A LOT of compost quickly—more than you can make in your backyard—or if you haven't yet been inspired to start a backyard pile but want to feed the soil in your garden, you can use commercially produced compost. This compost is likely to be on sale in bags at your local garden center, or you may be able to load a bunch into plastic bags in the back of your car or truck at your local composting operation. With a little research, you should be able to find a reliable, consistent supply of excellent compost somewhere near you.

Commercially produced compost is made from a variety of organics—the leaves and brush collected from yards around the country each fall, the biosolids or "sewage sludge" that has long posed a disposal problem for most municipalities, or the manure from the animals that provide us with milk, eggs, meat and other products. Even industrial wastes such as food-processing residues are becoming more common in compost recipes.

Not too long ago, most of these compostables would have headed straight to the landfill, but the number of landfills has decreased in the last couple of decades, and municipalities have been under pressure to cut waste disposal costs. Among the sound solutions they've chosen is composting. Compostables are no small potato in the waste stream; in many urban areas they make up 60 percent of the total. Yard trimmings alone are 20 percent of the U.S. waste

Many municipalities collect yard waste or have sites where people can drop theirs off.

stream. This eminently recyclable fraction of our waste is now widely composted. In 1996, 3,500 yard-waste composting programs across the country were processing 8 million tons of yard trimmings yearly.

You can obtain most commercial composts produced locally from either a dealer in your area—a garden center, topsoil dealer, mulch dealer, nursery or landscaper—or from your local composting facility.

How composts made of different materials affect different kinds of plants in different types of soils is still a largely unexplored area. But with some experimentation, you can determine how various composts best benefit your garden. Below you'll find some help sorting out the commercial composts that are available and where they might best be used. You can also contact your local Cooperative Extension office for information about the commercial compost suppliers in your area.

COMPOSTS MADE FROM YARD TRIMMINGS

The compost you'll most readily find is made from yard trimmings or leaves. Many cities gather leaves each fall using either a leaf vacuum or another collection device, depositing them at a local "leaf dump," or commercial composting center. Workers there grind the brush and woody materials into a fine mulch-grade product, then place it into windrows (long piles, triangular in cross-section), where it composts. Most commercial yard-trimming facilities in temperate climates produce a good quality compost in three to six months.

Sites that collect only leaves skip the grinding process altogether and simply put leaves into windrows to produce "leaf mold." Most commercial facilities limit the amount of wood in each mixture to less than 30 percent because the woody fraction takes longer to break down. If a compost facility uses a high percentage of woody materials in the mix, it will produce a "mulchier" or coarser final product, but one that also contains a lot of organic matter.

Make sure that the compost you buy has been screened to at most 1-inch size pieces, but preferably to a ½-inch grade. You'll find that the more finely screened compost has more applications in your yard, from topdressing the lawn to enhancing the soil in a flower bed.

Unlike fertilizers, most yard-trimming composts don't contain lots of highly soluble nutrients. They may have an N-P-K ratio as low as 1-1-1. But these balanced composts slowly release their nutrients over time, and won't burn tender plant roots. By using compost, which helps soil hold onto nutrients, you can cut back on or eliminate soluble fertilizers, depending on your climate, soil type and type of plants you grow.

Yard-trimming composts are normally reasonably priced in bulk at local supply centers; you'll generally find them for $15 to $30 per cubic yard. If you have a regional composting site, you'll find bulk compost there at a lower cost, or for free.

COMPOST MADE FROM BIOSOLIDS

Municipalities have found that disposing of "biosolids," or sewage sludge, is among the toughest waste disposal problems around. But composted biosolids have found a receptive audience among gardeners and landscapers, and the process is an increasingly popular way to transform what was once a problem into some of the best compost available on the market today.

Many cities operate large-scale sites where they compost sewage sludge.

Biosolids are little more than "human manure," and, like animal manures, are highly regulated because they have the potential to pass pathogens from person to person. Both states and the federal government have passed regulations designed to ensure that the levels of pathogens and heavy metals are well within the human and animal safety guidelines established by the Environmental Protection Agency.

Because they are highly regulated, biosolids composts are normally consistent in quality, high in nutrients and dependable in supply. Many facilities operate seven days a week and may not change recipes for many years. Some facilities have sold out of their compost every year since they opened.

Most composting facilities combine biosolids with woody materials that have been shredded or ground to a fine mulch size. Biosolids are very wet

Milwaukee's biosolid-based compost is sold widely as Milorganite.

and wood is normally quite dry; the resulting mixture is easily piled into windrows. The nitrogen in the biosolids helps break down the woody materials and the wood adds structure to the mixture.

Biosolids composts can include any number of bulking agents, which lend different appearances and uses to the finished compost. When composters use wood chips, the end product is coarser; if your garden has a compacted clay soil, this is the compost for you. Use compost bulked with sawdust or finely ground wood to topdress established turf after you have aerated it. Find out what type of biosolids compost you're getting before purchasing, and ask for directions on use.

Biosolids compost often has a slight odor, which is indicative of the age of the material. If the odor is unbearable, the compost has probably not aged enough and could harm plants. If the odor is only slight, it is most likely aged and ready for the garden. Let your nose be your guide to selecting a high quality product.

COMPOSTS MADE FROM ANIMAL MANURES

Animal manures are an excellent source of organic matter, and were the basis of the first composts humans made. They remain popular today; cow and chicken manures are the best-sellers. Make sure that the manure you are getting has been composted—dehydrated cow manure is also available and is less beneficial for the soil. Composted cow manures and biosolids compost have roughly the

continues on page 100

SHOPPING TIPS: HOW TO CHOOSE THE BEST COMMERCIAL COMPOST

R un the compost through your hands. Does it smell earthy, like soil? If so, it is stable and ready for use. If it smells vinegary or of ammonia it needs to compost more. As you run your hands through it, make sure that it is not hot to the touch; this compost also needs to age further. A fully finished compost will be the same temperature as the air.

Look at the compost color. Most composts that are ready to be used are very dark brown to black, and are a consistent color throughout the compost pile. (There are some exceptions to this rule. Chicken manure compost, for example, is normally lighter in color.)

Buy compost with a fertilizer analysis (N-P-K value) of at least 1-.5-.5, to 1-1-1. The numbers may look low but the compost will release more nutrients over time and you will be adding organic matter to the soil.

Ask your supplier if the levels of soluble salts in the compost have been tested. These levels could be important, depending on the type of plants you plan to grow (salt levels should be at least below 5 mmhos/cm). Many tender annuals are salt sensitive; they do not transplant well and suffer from what is called "transplanting shock"—actually a slight burn from the salts. Make sure that the soluble salts in the compost fall below the level deemed safe for the plants you intend to use.

The original ingredients that went into the compost should be nearly unrecognizable. If the compost is made from leaves, you shouldn't see half of a leaf in the finished compost. Likewise, if the compost is made from twigs and branches, none should be visible after the product has been screened for sale.

If you plan to buy compost in bulk, consider asking your supplier the following questions. Do you provide directions for proper use of the compost for my specific needs? Is a steady, consistent supply on hand at all times? Has the product been tested and if so, are the test results available? Has the compost been used in any local projects—demonstration plots, university research programs or award-winning landscapes? Can you custom mix compost so that it fills my needs?

HOW MUCH COMPOST DO I NEED?

To determine how much compost you'll need to amend different parts of the garden and yard, measure the square footage of the areas you plan to add compost to. Then consult "How Much Compost to Use in the Garden?" on page 93. It shows how deep a layer of compost you should apply to different areas and for various uses in the garden. Line up the depth of compost you need (across) with the square footage (down) to find the number of cubic yards of compost you'll need.

CUBIC YARDS REQUIRED PER AREA

SQUARE FEET	¼"	½"	1"	1½"	2"
100	0.08	0.16	0.32	0.48	0.62
500	0.40	0.80	1.60	2.40	3.10
1,000	0.80	1.60	3.20	4.80	6.20
3,000	2.40	4.80	9.60	14.40	18.60
5,000	4.00	8.00	16.00	24.00	31.00
10,000	8.00	16.00	32.00	48.00	62.00
15,000	12.00	24.00	48.00	72.00	93.00

Source: Rod Tyler, 1996

same N-P-K levels—about 1-1-1 or 2-1-1. The nutrients in chicken manure compost, which has N-P-K levels from 2-2-2 to 5-2-2, are usually much more readily available. If the chicken manure is well composted, you need not fear that the compost will burn your plants as *un*composted chicken manure can. The compost releases nutrients slowly over the entire growing season.

If you live in a suburban or urban area, you may find that composts made from animal manures are more expensive than leaf compost or biosolids compost produced locally. The expense of transporting small bulk quantities of gardening products made from manures to the city increases their overall cost.

COMPOST MADE FROM MUNICIPAL SOLID WASTE

Municipal Solid Waste (MSW) compost is made chiefly from a jumble of solid waste—compostable materials as well as non-compostables. The fraction that

A large proportion of the stuff we send to landfills is compostable. As landfills like New York City's Fresh Kills (above) close, composting makes more and more sense.

does not compost is sifted out of the finished compost. But MSW compost does not usually look as good as the composts described above—it can contain small pieces of glass, plastic and other materials that pass through the screens and remain in the final product.

Although a lot of research has been conducted demonstrating the safety and benefits of the MSW compost, it has not found a big following among the gardening public. You probably won't find bags of MSW compost at your local garden center. If you are interested in buying MSW compost, contact a nearby vendor and ask for a representative sample before you place your order.

SPECIALTY COMPOSTS

Compost producers have begun to make specialty composts, a trend that is just beginning to catch on. You can already find composts made to suppress specific plant diseases, which have only been controllable in the past with pesticides. You may soon find products made for specific plant families, like acidified compost for rhododendrons and azaleas or high-nitrogen compost for turf topdressing. The recipes for these specialty products are limited only by the needs of the marketplace.

101

RESOURCES

FURTHER READING

Compost!: Growing Gardens from Your Garbage, Linda Glaser, Millbrook Press, Brookfield, CT, 1996 (a family activity book)

Cover Crop Gardening: Soil Enrichment with Green Manures, Storey Publishing Bulletin A-5, Story Communications, Pownal, VT, 1977

Easy Composting, editorial staff of Ortho Books, Ortho Books, San Ramon, CA, 1992

Fertile Soil: A Grower's Guide to Organic and Inorganic Fertilizers, Robert Parnes, agAccess, Davis, CA, 1990

Fertilizer for Free, Charles Siegchrist, Storey Publishing Bulletin A-44, Storey Communications, Pownal, VT, 1980

From the Good Earth, Michael Ableman, Harry N. Abrams, Inc, New York, NY, 1993

Handbook of Ecological Lawn Care, Paul D. Sachs, The Edaphic Press, Newbury, VT, 1996

Improving Your Soil, Storey Publishing Bulletin A-20, Storey Communications, Pownal, VT, 1980

Let it Rot!, Stu Campbell, Garden Way Publishing, 1975

Make Compost in 14 Days, the editors of *Organic Gardening* magazine, Rodale Press, Emmaus, PA, 1982

The Mulch Book: A Complete Guide for Gardeners, Stu Campbell, Storey Communications, Pownal, VT, 1991

Organic Gardening, Geoff Hamilton, editor, Reader's Digest, Pleasantville, NY, 1992

Pay Dirt: Farming and Gardening with Composts, J.I. Rodale, The Devin-Adair Co., New York, NY, 1946

Rodale Book of Composting, Deborah L. Martin and Grace Gershuny, editors, St. Martin's Press, New York, NY, 1992

Start with the Soil, Grace Gershuny, Rodale Press, Emmaus, PA, 1997

Worms Eat My Garbage, Mary Appelhof, Flower Press, Kalamazoo, MI, 2nd edition, 1997

COMPOSTING ONLINE

I f you have access to the World Wide Web, you'll find lots of information about composting, and discussions among composters who need help and others who have answers. For in-depth information about backyard composting start with the Cornell University site, Cornell Composting. The address of the site is http://www.cals.cornell.edu/dept/compost

Another good site, especially for urban composters, is City Farmer, Canada's Office of Urban Agriculture. This site has excellent information about growing food and composting in cities. City Farmer's address is http://www.cityfarmer.org

If you want to get into a conversation with other composters, where you can raise questions about your pile and get answers from experienced composters, try the forum on the Composting Resource website at http://www.oldgrowth.org/compost/index.html

The Brooklyn Botanic Garden also has a wonderful website (http://www.bbg.org) that includes a wealth of information about composting, with an emphasis on urban composting. The site also includes a schedule of composting classes that are held at the garden on a regular basis.

Websites do sometimes vanish without a trace or change addresses without notification, and new ones open up all the time. To find what's currently on the web, use one of the many search engines such as Alta Vista or Yahoo! Or you can subscribe to a listserve (see the Cornell site for directions on how to subscribe), which will include you in an ongoing conversation among composters.

BROOKSTONE COMPANY
1655 Bassford Drive
Mexico, MO 65256
800-926-7000
compost bins

FLOWERFIELD ENTERPRISES
10332 Shaver Rd.
Kalamazoo, MI 49024
616-327-0108
worms, worm bins

GARDENER'S SUPPLY COMPANY
128 Intervale Road
Burlington, VT 05401-2850
800-863-1700
*compost bins, bioactivator, aerating
tools, kitchen waste collectors, worms,
worm bins, finished compost*

NATURAL GARDENING COMPANY
217 Anselmo Avenue
San Anselmo, CA 94960
415-456-5060
*leaf shredder, compost bins,
bioactivator, aerating tools, kitchen
waste collectors, worms, worm bins,
compost sifters*

NATURE'S BACKYARD
241 Duchaine Blvd.
New Bedford, MA 02745
800-853-2525
compost bins

NORSEMAN PLASTICS
2296 Kenmore Ave.

Buffalo, NY 14207
800-267-4391
compost bins

PEACEFUL VALLEY FARM SUPPLY
P.O. Box 2209
Grass Valley, CA 95945
916-272-4769
*compost bins, bioactivator, aerating
tools, thermometers, worms, worm bins,
compost sifters*

PLOW AND HEARTH
P.O. Box 5000
Madison, VA 22727-1500
800-627-1712
*compost bins, bioactivator, kitchen
waste collectors, worms, worm bins*

REACH INC.
P.O. Box 1748
Klamath Falls, OR 97601
503-882-8803
compost bins

RECyCAL SUPPLY CO.
P.O. Box 377
Murrieta, CA 92564
800-927-3873
compost bins

RECYCLED PLASTIC COMPANY
2829 152ND AVE. NE
Redmond, WA 98052
425-867-3200
compost bins

SEEDS OF CHANGE
P.O. Box 15700
Santa Fe, NM 87506
888-762-7333
compost bins, bioactivator, aerating tools, thermometers, worms, worm bins

SEVENTH GENERATION
49 Hercules Drive
Colchester, VT 05446
802-655-6777
compost bins

SMITH AND HAWKEN
117 East Strawberry Drive
Mill Valley, CA 94941
800-776-3336
compost bins, worms, worm bins, kitchen waste collectors

SNOW POND FARM SUPPLY
RR2 Box 1009
Belgrade, ME 04917
800-768-9998
bioactivator, aerating tools, kitchen waste collectors, worms, worm bins

TROY BILT/GARDEN WAY
102nd Street and 9th Ave.
Troy, NY 12180
800-833-6990
compost bins, chipper-shredders

VERMITECHNOLOGY UNLIMITED
P.O. Box 130
Orange Lake, FL 32681
worms

WE RECYCLE CORP.
19-342 Bronte St.
S. Milton, Ontario
L9T5B7 Canada
416-875-2588
compost bins

WILLINGHAM WORM FARM
Rt. 1, Box 241
Butler, GA 31006
worms

THE UNIVERSITY OF MASSACHUSETTS COOPERATIVE EXTENSION SERVICE now has **a mail-order compost testing service;** they'll test for extractable major and minor plant nutrients, moisture content, pH, organic matter, total nitrogen, nitrate, ammonium, carbon-to-nitrogen ratio, soluble salts, and extractable heavy metals. Phone the lab (413-545-2311) before mailing samples. Send each sample, with a check or money order for $20 payable to "UMass," to UMass Soil Test Laboratory, West Experiment Station, North Pleasant St., University of Massachusetts, Amherst, MA 01003. Include a note outlining the compost's original ingredients, length of aging and projected use.

CONTRIBUTORS

MARY APPELHOF, a biologist and educator in Kalamazoo, Michigan, is the author of *Worms Eat My Garbage* as well as numerous articles on solid-waste topics. She is the founder of Flowerfield Enterprises, a company that sells worm bins and worms for composting.

GRACE GERSHUNY is the author of several books and articles on soil management and composting, including *Start with the Soil,* published in 1997 by Rodale Press; she was editor of *Organic Farmer: The Digest of Sustainable Agriculture* for its four-year existence. Gershuny lives in Barnet, Vermont and serves on the faculty of Goddard College and the Institute for Social Ecology.

BENJAMIN GRANT is former instructor for the Brooklyn Botanic Garden's Urban Composting Project. He has taught courses in composting and environmental issues to children, adults and landscape professionals. He has a B.A. in Environmental Studies from Columbia University and is currently enrolled in the urban design program at U.C. Berkeley.

BETH HANSON is managing editor of the Brooklyn Botanic Garden's 21st Century Gardening Series and former managing editor of the Natural Resource Defense Council's *Amicus Journal.* She writes about gardening and environmental issues for a variety of publications and composts just north of New York City.

PATRICIA JASAITIS is coordinator of Brooklyn Botanic Garden's Urban Composting Project, a joint educational initiative with the New York City Department of Sanitation. She has also worked in community gardening with the Green Guerrillas in Manhattan and in urban forestry at the Morris Arboretum in Philadelphia.

JOSEPH KEYSER is the educational specialist for Montgomery County, Maryland's Department of Environmental Protection. In 1995 Keyser won the the Composting Council's H. Clark Gregory Award for Outstanding Grassroots Efforts to Promote Composting. Keyser writes the "Green Page" column for Gazette newspapers.

MIRANDA SMITH has been teaching organic horticulture and farming to gardeners and commercial farmers since 1971. She currently teaches at the New

England Small Farm Institute in Belchertown, Massachusetts. Smith is author of several books on gardening, including *Your Backyard Herb Garden* and *Backyard Fruits and Berries,* both published by Rodale Press.

ROD TYLER, a former vice president of the Composting Council and active member of the council's marketing committee, has written dozens of articles about the making and marketing of compost.

JEFF WILKINSON is an architect in Beacon, NY, where he heads his own design firm. He teaches furniture design at the New York School of Interior Design. His illustrations have appeared in numerous publications including *The Naturally Elegant Home* (Little-Brown, 1993) and the *New York Times*. He serves the city of Beacon as chairman of the Conservation Advisory Committee.

ILLUSTRATION CREDITS

SAXON HOLT: cover, pages 4, 20, 36 bottom, 37, 42 top, 43 bottom, 59 bottom, 60 bottom, 61, 64 bottom, 65, and 85.

DAVID CAVAGNARO: pages 1, 18, 33 bottom, 50, 67, 87, and 92.

JUDYWHITE: pages 7, 15, 19, 38, 39 left and right, 41, 49 bottom, 64 top, 66, 68, 72, 90, 91, 94.

MT. VERNON LADIES ASSOCIATION: page 10 left and right.

MICHAEL ABLEMAN: page 13.

DANIEL L. DINDAL: pages 21, 23 top, center and bottom, and 24 left and right.

LIZ BALL: pages 25, 26, 27, 29, 36 center, 42 bottom, 43 top, 45, 49 top, 58 top left, bottom center, 59 top left, 60 top, 63, and 97.

DEREK FELL: pages 17, 32 top, and 86.

CHRISTINE DOUGLAS: 32 bottom, 33 top, 36 top, 58 top right, bottom left, 62 left, 81, and 84 left and right.

TORO: page 44.

SCOTT VLAUN: pages 58 top center, 62 right, and 71.

PATRICIA JASAITIS: pages 58 bottom right, 82, 83, and 101.

ALAN DETRICK: 59 top right, and 96.

ROBIN TENCH: page 69.

KITCHEN GARDEN MAGAZINE: pages 73, 74, 75 top and bottom, 77 top and bottom, and 79.

BETH HANSON: page 98.

INDEX

Brooklyn Botanic Garden
21st-Century Gardening Series

BROOKLYN BOTANIC GARDEN
NATIVE PERENNIALS
North American Beauties

21ST-CENTURY GARDENING SERIES
BROOKLYN BOTANIC GARDEN
TANTALIZING TOMATOES
Smart Tips & Tasty Picks
for Gardeners Everywhere

BROOKLYN BOTANIC GARDEN
SALAD GARDENS
Gourmet Greens
and Beyond

BROOKLYN BOTANIC GARDEN
BULBS FOR INDOORS
Year-round
Windowsill Splendor

BROOKLYN BOTANIC GARDEN
NATURAL INSECT CONTROL
The Ecological Gardener's
Guide to Foiling Pests

For further information please contact the Brooklyn Botanic Garden
1000 Washington Avenue   Brooklyn, New York 11225   (718) 622-4433 ext. 265   www.bbg.org